REAL ESTATE IN INDIA

AN INTRODUCTION TO THE MARKET, TRENDS, VALUATIONS & INVESTING STRATEGIES

GURCHARAN KAURA

To my Mom, Dad & Rajveer!

Contents

Preface

Real Estate in India: An Introduction to the Market, Trends, Valuations & Investing Strategies explains about the Indian Real Estate Market. Indian Real Estate market is going to be $1 trillion by 2030, and I truly believe that this decade is of Real Estate. There are many upcoming trends in the industry, Warehousing, Datacenters, Prop-Tech, The silver economy etc. about which I have told in this book. I have also given the overview of the Indian real estate sector right now and what is government's plan to achieve high success in this sector.

Apart from the market and the trends, I have also explained in this book some valuation methods to value a property, documentation part, REITs in very much detail, Business models of some companies which are working in this sector, Prop-Tech and some Indian Prop-Tech startups, some tips for buyers and sellers of the property, and most importantly some investing strategies which can make you a millionaire or a multi-millionaire. I have also explained the technical terms used in the real estate industry, RERA in India, and how to finance a house, how to start your prop-tech startup, how my own company works, this all things are also covered in very much detail in this book. And I have also touched upon some dark sides such as corruption in the real estate market and some lack of transparency, so that you can get a complete overview about this industry. And I am sure, if you have an interest in real estate market, then, you are going to gain some very useful insights from this book, and you will love this book!

What this book covers,

Chapter 1, Real Estate Jargon, Financing and Regulations, explains about many technical terms used in the real estate industry and their meanings with real-life examples. Then I talked about RERA Act in India, 2016 and some regulations for builders set up by RERA and how RERA has transformed this industry from an unorganized sector to an organized and regulated industry, then I have told about the number of various options for a person to finance a home in India and what all is required to get a loan and steps required.

Chapter 2, Real Estate and Property Valuations, covers the most used six methods for valuing a property in India. These are Comparable Sales

Approach, Cost Approach, Income Capitalization method, Sales Comparison Approach, Hybrid and Residual method, Automated Valuation model as well. I have explained them in much detail, with real-life examples and in this chapter, I have also talked about some ownership types and property types and explained them in an easy language.

Chapter 3, Property Documentation, covers all the documents which are required to buy or sell a property, or which documents you should check before buying and investing in a property. I have talked about them in much detail, then I also talked about some frauds which are happening in this industry with common people and how you can save yourself from these frauds.

Chapter 4, How to become a Real Estate Millionaire Investor, covers nine to ten investing strategies which millionaires use to make money, These are Fix-and-Flip, Buy-and-Hold, Wholesaling, Development, BRRRR, Turnkey, House Hacking, Student Rental, Vacation Rental strategies. I have covered all of them in much detail with some examples as well, and then I also told about the number of possible occupations in the real estate industry to make good money, and how to become a builder, broker and I also shared in this chapter, how I did this and most importantly, I also discussed how you can apply these strategies with zero money down or without investing your any money, and how to network, find investors, these tips are also shared in this chapter.

Chapter 5, Real Estate Investment Trusts (REITs), covers everything related to REITs. Starting from defining what are REITs to their key features and characteristics, to their benefits and then defining some terms like NAV, WALE, occupancy rate etc. to analyzing REITs and selecting good ones. I told here about the three Indian REITs as well and some regulatory aspects as well, I covered here. Then I also gave my view on present and future of REITs in India.

Chapter 6, Let's Explore Prop-Tech, covers what is prop-tech with examples. Here, I covered some companies and Indian startups who are doing good in this segment and how Prop-Tech is enabling Real Estate market with technology. And then I also gave you some tips how to start your own startup in Prop-Tech and I also discussed the business models of some good prop-tech startups in our country like NoBroker, PropTiger, MagicBricks as well.

Chapter 7, Business models of some companies working in Real Estate, covers the business models of world's biggest four real estate companies like Brookfield, Blackstone etc. Then I discussed some Indian companies doing good in this sector i.e. DLF, Godrej Properties etc. Then I showed McDonald's balance sheet and told how McDonald's is a real estate company. Then, I discussed some construction companies' business model. I talked about world's largest company in this sector, i.e. Ferrovial and then some Indian companies in this sector as well, Reliance Infra, Hindustan Construction Company and the TATA group etc.

Chapter 8, **Some Tips for Buying and Selling a Property**, covers about some tips which you can take care while buying a property and then some tips for the sellers of the property so that they can get the right value for their property.

Chapter 9, Corruption in Indian Real Estate market, covers about some dark side of the Indian Real Estate market that how the big and corrupt people use their black money in real estate market and how this leads to un-affordability of houses for a common man. How this practice artificially inflate prices of homes and flats.

Chapter 10, Renting vs Buying a property, covers both the financial view and the emotional view to help you decide whether you should buy or rent a property. I also talked about the general pros and cons of both renting and buying, and I think this chapter will make you able to decide what should you do.

Chapter 11, Overview and Future trends of Real Estate sector in India, covers the present situation of real estate in India. Here, in this chapter, I completely analyze the real estate sector fundamentally, and I told here about the long real estate cycles, from 2013-14, to what happened during Covid-19 pandemic in real estate market, how due to our good and helpful government policies, it became blessing in disguise for real estate sector. And what is the current state of this sector, why 2023 is the best time to enter into real estate sector and how climate change, silver economy will impact this sector. I also discussed some most promising future trends, including Datacenters, Warehousing to Blockchain, then I also talked about the differences between the real estate industries of the USA, the Canada, the Dubai and our India and how this decade is going to look like for this sector in India. Then, I also talked about which segments of the industry are in demand right now.

Chapter 12, Different Asset Classes and their comparison with Real Estate, covers about all the different asset classes present in the world right now, and I also arranged them in an order from the lowest risky to the highest risky, and then I showed the comparison of Real Estate as an asset with other asset classes on the basis of risk and return. At last, I also told you about how much of your portfolio should consist of Real Estate.

Acknowledgements

First and Foremost, I would like to express my sincere appreciation and gratitude to **Mr. Nitesh Bansal**, I learned discipline and my most of the core finance concepts got cleared because of him. He is an amazing teacher and my inspiration. I'd also like to express my appreciation to **my mom, dad, my sisters and Rajveer and my teachers at TIET** without whose support, encouragement, this book would never have been written.

Thanks, also, to my institute **Thapar Institute of Engineering and Technology**, who provide me with these opportunities. Thanks, also, to **all my friends at R.S. Model and TIET**, for their extremely valuable support.

Special thanks to **Mr. Nitin Gupta**, my senior at TIET.

And Thanks to all those real estate enthusiasts, with whom I worked, I learned so much from you **Mr. Anurag Sharma, Mr. Himanshu, Mr. Pankaj and Mr. Anupam**. You all helped me sharpen my understanding of real estate industry.

CHAPTER ONE

Real Estate Jargon, Financing and Regulations (RERA)

Brush Up your Real Estate Jargon:

In this introductory chapter, I will introduce you with some most used terms in Real-Estate Industry, and before we start our journey of analyzing Indian real estate market, you should have a basic idea of these terms because these terms will be used by me in next chapters. So, let's begin:

The first in the list is **Carpet Area**, It refers to the actual area of a building or apartment that can be covered by a carpet. It is the area within the walls of a building, including the area of the rooms, but not including the thickness of the walls. It is the area that is available for use and is generally smaller than the built-up area or super built-up area. Carpet area is measured in square feet and is used to calculate the area of a property for the purpose of buying, renting, or selling. It is also used to calculate the property tax, stamp duty, and registration fees. Carpet area does not include the area covered by the common areas like corridors, staircases, lobbies, lifts, etc. It also does not include the area covered by the walls, balconies, and terraces.

Carpet area is considered to be the most accurate measure of the usable area of a property, and it is generally used as a benchmark for pricing and valuation of properties. It is also used to compare properties with similar floor plans, regardless of the location or construction quality.

Second is, **Built-up area** refers to the total area of a building or apartment that includes the carpet area, as well as the area covered by the walls, corridors, staircases, balconies, and terraces. It is the area that is enclosed by the outer walls of a building and includes the area of the rooms, bathrooms, kitchens, and other spaces. Built-up area is measured in square feet and is also used to calculate the area of a property for the purpose of buying, renting, or selling. It can also be used to calculate the property tax, stamp duty, and registration fees. Built-up area is generally larger than the carpet area because it includes the area covered by the walls, balconies, and terraces. However, it does not include the area covered by common areas like corridors, staircases, lobbies, lifts, etc.

Built-up area is a broader measure of the area of a property, and it is also used as a benchmark for pricing and valuation of properties. However, it's less accurate in terms of usable area, as it includes the area covered by the walls, balconies, and terraces.

Third is, **Super Built-up Area**, used to refer to the total area of a building or apartment that includes the carpet area, as well as the area covered by the walls, corridors, staircases, balconies, terraces, and also common areas like lift, lobby, swimming pool, clubhouse and other amenities that are available for the use of all residents. Super Built-up Area is generally larger than the carpet area or built-up area, as it includes the area covered by common areas like corridors, staircases, lobbies, lifts, etc. It can also be used to calculate the area of a property for the purpose of buying, renting, or selling.

Super Built-up area is considered to be the most inflated measure of the area of a property, as it includes the area covered by common areas that are not always available for use by the residents and also not considered as usable area. It is generally used by developers and builders to inflate the area of a property and charge more for it.

Next in the list is, **Floor Space Index (FSI)**, is a measure used to determine the maximum built-up area that can be constructed on a plot of land. It is calculated as the ratio of the total built-up area on a plot of land to the total area of the plot. The FSI varies depending on the location, zoning, and other factors. In India, the FSI is set by local authorities and can vary from city to city and even within different areas within a city.

For example, in Mumbai, the FSI for residential areas is generally 1.33, meaning that a 1,000 square meter plot of land can have a maximum built-up area of 1,330 square meters. In commercial areas, the FSI is generally higher, such as 2.5, meaning that a 1,000 square meter plot of land can have a maximum built-up area of 2,500 square meters. The FSI is used as a tool to control urbanization and development, and to ensure that the density of population and buildings in an area is sustainable.

Next is, **Floor Area Ratio (FAR),** is another measure used in India to determine the maximum built-up area that can be constructed on a plot of land. It is similar to Floor Space Index (FSI), but it is calculated as the ratio of the total built-up area on a plot of land to the total area of the plot and the area of the open spaces that are required to be provided like gardens and open spaces. The FAR is another tool which is used to control urbanization and development and to ensure that the density of population and buildings in an area is sustainable. Similarly, The FAR, as well, is set by local authorities, and it can vary from city to city and even within different areas within a city.

For example, in Mumbai, the FAR for residential areas is generally 1.33 (You will observe that It is the same as that of FSI because the formula for calculating FAR and FSI is almost the same), meaning that a 1,000 square meter plot of land can have a maximum built-up area of 1,330 square meters, and the open spaces should be provided accordingly (In this, included). In commercial areas, the FAR is generally higher, such as 2.5, meaning that a 1,000 square meter plot of land can have a maximum built-up area of 2,500 square meters, and the open spaces should be provided accordingly (Included here).

It's important to note that, FSI and FAR are not exactly same, FSI is the ratio of built-up area to the area of the plot only, whereas, FAR is the ratio of the built-up area to the area of the plot and the open spaces.

Next we have is, **Circle rate**, refers to the minimum price at which a property can be sold or registered in a particular area. This rate is determined by the government and is based on the location and type of property. We will talk about this in detail in our Corruptions in Real Estate Industry chapter, there I will tell you how the big giants of the Industry use this circle rate.

In addition, **Ready Reckoner rate**, is the rate at which property is valued for the purpose of stamp duty and registration charges.

Next we have are, **Lease**, a legal agreement that allows a tenant to use a property for a specified period of time. **Leasehold property**, refers to a property that is owned by someone for a certain number of years and then returned to the original owner. Leasehold properties are typically used for commercial properties. **Freehold property** is a property which is owned outright and can be sold or transferred without any restrictions.

Appreciation, an increase in the value of a property over time. **Depreciation**, a decrease in the value of a property over time. **Equity**, the difference between the value of a property and the amount of debt outstanding on the property. **Capitalization rate**, a measure of the potential return on an investment property. **Broker**, a licensed professional who helps buyers and sellers with real estate transactions. **Commission**, the fee paid to a real estate agent for their services. **Contingency**, a condition that must be met before a sale can be completed. **Counteroffer**, a revised offer made by the seller in response to an initial offer. **Escrow**, a neutral third party that holds funds or documents until certain conditions are met. **Foreclosure**, the process of taking possession of a property due to the borrower's failure to make loan payments. **Open house**, an event where a property is open to the public for viewing. **Home inspection**, a professional examination of a property to identify any potential issues. **Homeowners association (HOA)**, a group that manages a community of properties. **Comparable sale**, a recent sale of a similar property in the same area. **Lien**, a legal claim on a property to secure payment of a debt. **Listing**, a property that is for sale or rent. **Lock-box**, a secure container used to hold the key to a property for easy access by real estate agents. **Home loan, or Mortgage loan**, refers to a loan taken from a bank or other financial institution to purchase a property. **Principal**, the amount of money borrowed on a loan, not including interest. **Interest rate**, the percentage of interest charged on a loan. **EMI, or Equated Monthly Installments**, refers to the fixed amount that a borrower pays to the lender each month to repay a loan. **Mortgage broker**, a licensed professional who helps borrowers find the best mortgage loan. **Origination fee**, a fee charged by a lender for processing a loan application. **Credit score**, a measure of a person's creditworthiness. Default - failure to make loan payments. **Loan to value (LTV) ratio**, is a financial term used by banks and NBFCs. It is the ratio of the loan amount to the value of the property. Banks usually have LTV ratios set for different types of properties, and the LTV ratio can affect the interest rate of the loan. **Refinance**, refers to the process of obtaining a new mortgage to replace an existing one, usually with the aim of obtaining a lower interest rate or changing the terms of the loan. **Pre-approval**, a letter from a lender indicating that a borrower is pre-approved for a loan. **Owner financing**, a type of financing in which the seller of a property provides financing for the buyer. **Property registration**, refers to the process of officially recording the transfer of a property from one person to another. It is a legal requirement in India and is done at the office of the sub-registrar of the area where the property is located. **Down payment**, refers to the initial payment made by a buyer to the seller at the time of purchase. It is typically a percentage of the total purchase price. **Property registration**, refers to the process of officially recording the transfer of a property from one person to another. It is a legal requirement in India and is done at the office of the sub-registrar of the area where the property is located. **Power of attorney**, refers to a legal document that gives one person the authority to act on behalf of another person. It is often used in real estate transactions to allow one person to sign documents and make decisions on behalf of another person. **Title search**, refers to the process of verifying the legal ownership of a property. A title search is typically done before purchasing a property to ensure that there are no outstanding claims or liens on the property. **Encumbrance certificate**, a document that confirms that a property is free from any legal or financial liabilities. It is issued by the office of the sub-registrar and is valid for a period of 30 days from the date of issue. **Home insurance**, refers to the insurance policy that covers the structure of the house, its contents, and personal liability. It protects the homeowner from any financial loss due to natural calamities, fire, theft, or other unforeseen incidents. **Closing**, refers to the final step in a real estate transaction, in which the sale of a property is completed, and the title is transferred to the buyer. **Closing costs**, refers to the various expenses that a buyer and seller must pay in order to complete a real estate transaction. These can include things like attorney's fees, title insurance, and property taxes. **GST, or Goods and Services Tax**, is a value-added tax that is applied to all goods and services in India. GST is applicable on all real estate transactions. **Zoning**, refers to the regulation of the use of land within a certain area, determining what can be built and how it can be used. These are some of the most important and most used terms in the Real Estate Industry in India currently. There are some terms here related to financing of real estate, some are related to regulations and some are other technical terms (Related to area, floors, documents, price, types etc.) Now, we will discuss in this introductory chapter more regarding regulations and financing (especially by loan) in the Real Estate Industry in India.

Regulations in Real Estate Sector in India

Real estate was a very much unorganized and unregulated sector before 2015-16, There were many problems in that. Builders were not delivering projects on their said deadlines, some frauds were also happening with common man etc. Then in this unregulated market, there comes RERA, and it just transformed this market into a regulated market with its regulations and oversight on builders and developers in the real estate sector in India. Now, you will be wondering what is RERA, and how it did this? Let's see everything in detail:

The **Real Estate (Regulation and Development) Act, 2016 (RERA)** is a central legislation in India that regulates the real estate sector and aims to protect the rights of buyers and promoters. The Act applies to all residential and commercial projects that have been launched on or after May 1, 2017, and requires all developers to register their projects with the regulatory authority set up under the Act, known as the Real Estate Regulatory Authority (RERA).

One of the key objectives of RERA is to ensure transparency and accountability in the real estate sector. Under the Act, developers are required to disclose all details of the project, including the layout plan, land status, and details of approvals obtained, to the RERA. They are also required to disclose the status of construction, including the completion date, to buyers and investors. RERA also aims to protect the rights of buyers by ensuring that developers adhere to the terms of the agreement and deliver the property on time. Under the Act, developers are not allowed to make any changes to the project without the prior written consent of two-thirds of the buyers. In the event of a delay in completion, developers are liable to pay an interest to buyers, and in case of default, the developers can be penalized, or their registration can be cancelled. The Act also provides for an appellate tribunal to hear appeals from decisions made by the RERA, and also provides for the establishment of a state-level regulatory authority for each state. The state-level authorities are responsible for enforcing the provisions of the Act within their respective states, and have the power to investigate and prosecute any violations of the Act.

In addition to these provisions, RERA also requires developers to maintain a separate account for each project, and to use the funds collected from buyers only for the construction of that specific project. This ensures that the funds collected from one project are not used for another project, thus protecting the buyers' interests.

In conclusion, RERA is a significant legislation that aims to bring transparency and accountability to the Indian real estate sector. By ensuring that developers adhere to the terms of the agreement and deliver the property on time, the Act aims to protect the rights of buyers and investors, and to promote the growth of the real estate sector in India.

The Real Estate Regulation and Development Act, 2016 (RERA) has several **key regulations** that developers must comply with in order to protect the rights of buyers and promote transparency and accountability in the real estate sector. Some of these key regulations include:

1. **Project registration:** Developers must register all residential and commercial projects with the Real Estate Regulatory Authority (RERA) before launching them. This registration process requires the developer to disclose detailed information about the project, including the layout plan, land status, and details of approvals obtained.

2. **Timely completion and delivery:** Developers must complete and deliver the project on time as per the agreement with the buyers. In the event of a delay, the developer must pay an interest to the buyers and can be penalized or have their registration cancelled in case of default.

3. **No changes to project without consent:** Developers are not allowed to make any changes to the project without the prior written consent of two-thirds of the buyers.

4. **Separate account for each project:** Developers must maintain a separate account for each project and use the funds collected from buyers only for the construction of that specific project.

5. **Disclosure of information:** Developers must disclose all information related to the project, including the status of construction, to buyers and investors.

6. **Grievance redressal mechanism:** RERA provides for an appellate tribunal and a state-level regulatory authority to hear appeals and investigate any violations of the Act.

7. **Adherence to laws and regulations:** Developers must comply with all relevant laws and regulations, including environmental laws, building codes, and zoning regulations.

8. **Homebuyer's protection:** RERA also provides for buyers protection by ensuring that the property is registered in their name and the developer should transfer all the rights and interests of the property to the allotted.

These regulations are designed to promote transparency, accountability, and fairness in the real estate sector and protect the rights of buyers. Developers who fail to comply with these regulations may face penalties or have their registration cancelled by RERA.

After seeing regulations, let's now see the ways of financing (via Loan) real estate in India :

1. Home loans: This is the most common form of financing for property purchase in India. A home loan is a type of loan that is specifically used to purchase a new home or to construct a new home. The loan is secured against the property, which means that the lender can take possession of the property if the borrower defaults on the loan. Banks and housing finance companies offer home loans at competitive interest rates. Home loans typically have a longer repayment period and lower interest rates compared to other types of loans.

2. Personal loans: Some individuals may use a personal loan to finance their property purchase. However, the interest rates on personal loans are generally higher than those on home loans.

3. Government schemes: The Government of India has launched several schemes to promote affordable housing, including the Pradhan Mantri Awas Yojana and the Credit-Linked Subsidy Scheme. These schemes offer financial assistance to eligible individuals for property purchase.

4. Co-applicant or Guarantor: Some Banks/ NBFC's in India also allows applicants to apply for a loan with a co-applicant or a guarantor, which can help increase the chances of loan approval and may also help in getting a better interest rate.

It is important to understand the terms and conditions, processing fee, interest rate, and other charges before availing any loan. It is also recommended to compare the loan offers from different providers and choose the one that best suits your needs and financial capacity.

Now, next, let's see, The steps required to apply and get a home loan in India:

1. Eligibility check: The first step is to check your eligibility for a home loan. This includes checking your credit score, income, and other factors that will determine whether you are eligible for a home loan and what the terms and conditions will be.

2. Choose a lender: Research different lenders and compare the interest rates, fees, and other terms and conditions to choose the lender that best suits your needs. First and second steps can be done simultaneously and after going through these, you finalize a particular lender, and it approves your eligibility and confirms that yes, you can repay the debt/loan.

3. Collect and submit the necessary documents: You will need to submit several documents, including proof of income, identity, and address, as well as property documents, to the lender.

4. Property evaluation: The lender will conduct an evaluation of the property to determine its value and ensure that it meets the lender's guidelines.

5. Approval and disbursal: Once the lender has reviewed your application and documents, they will approve the loan and disburse the funds to you.

6. Repayment: You will need to make regular repayment of the loan as per the terms and conditions agreed with the lender. (I know these are tough times, due to repo rate rise, your EMIs are increased (in case of floating-type interest rates (Mostly))).

It's important to have a good credit score and a stable source of income to increase the chances of loan approval. Also, it's important to compare the loan offers from different providers and choose the one that best suits your needs and financial capacity.

CHAPTER TWO

Real Estate and Property Valuations

So, before getting into real estate valuations, we must see some types and ownership structures of real estate and for what category, we will be seeing and doing property valuations.

Now, Real estate properties can be broadly categorized into several different types, based on their use and function. Some common types of properties include:

1. Residential properties: These properties are used for housing and can include single-family homes, townhouses, apartments, and condominiums.

2. Commercial properties: These properties are used for business and can include office buildings, retail space, industrial parks, and warehouses.

3. Industrial properties: These properties are used for manufacturing, production, and distribution. They can include factories, warehouses, and distribution centers.

4. Land: This can include vacant land, agricultural land, and land with special uses such as mining or forestry.

5. Mixed-use properties: These properties combine different types of uses, such as retail and residential or office and residential, into one development.

6. Hospitality properties: Hotels, Motels, Resorts, and other properties used for accommodation and hospitality.

7. Healthcare properties: Hospitals, clinics, nursing homes, assisted living facilities, and other properties used for healthcare services.

8. Special purpose properties: Properties built for specific use like schools, religious buildings, sports facilities, prisons, and other specialized properties.

This list is not exhaustive and there are many other types of properties that exist and being developed as per the need of the market. The type of property will determine the types of tenants who will be interested in renting or buying it, and it will also affect the property's value, cash flow and other financial characteristics.

Now, There are several different types of ownership and lease structures for real estate properties, including:

1. Fee simple ownership: This is the most common type of ownership, where an individual or entity holds legal title to the property and has the right to use, sell, or transfer it.

2. Leasehold ownership: This type of ownership occurs when an individual or entity holds the right to use a property for a specific period of time, as outlined in a lease agreement. At the end of the lease term, the property reverts back to the original owner.

3. Cooperative ownership: This type of ownership is common in multi-unit residential buildings, such as apartments. Under this structure, residents own shares in the building's corporation and have the right to occupy a specific unit.

4. Condominium ownership: Similar to Cooperative ownership, in condominium ownership, individual unit owners have the right to occupy and use a specific unit, but they own their units individually and share the ownership of the common areas of the building.

5. Tenancy in common: In this type of ownership, multiple parties own a property together and each party has an undivided interest in the property, which means each party can sell or transfer their interest without the consent of the other owners.

6. Joint tenancy: In this type of ownership is similar to tenancy in common, but with an important difference, it comes with a right of survivorship. This means that if one joint tenant dies, their interest in the property will pass automatically to the remaining joint tenants.

7. Lease: A legal agreement between a landlord and tenant, where the tenant pays rent to use the property for a specific period of time.

8. Ground Lease: A lease agreement in which a tenant rents land for a specific period of time, and construct a building or use it for specific purposes like farming, mining, etc.

9. Net Lease: A lease in which the tenant pays a base rent, as well as additional expenses such as property taxes, insurance, and maintenance costs.

10. Triple net lease: A lease in which the tenant pays base rent, as well as all operating expenses, taxes, insurance and maintenance costs of the property.

These are some of the common types of ownership and lease structures, but the specific terms and conditions can vary depending on the property and the parties involved. It is important to understand the specific terms and conditions of any property ownership or lease agreement before making a decision.

So, mostly in this book, you will see, I will be talking about residential and commercial properties more than any other type and that also mostly with fee-simple ownership type.

Now, we have got a basic idea, so let's start with property valuations. But before that, we must know why we need to do property valuations. So, let's see that first:

Why Property Valuations?

There could be different reasons for doing valuation of a property. Suppose you want to buy a property, so you would like to get the property at the right price, and you wouldn't want to overpay for it. Similarly, there is a seller who wants to sell his property. He will also want that he can get a maximum value for it. He does not want to sell his property undervalued. So, unless he knows the right value of his property, he will not know at which price he should sell it. Similarly, if you want to take insurance for a property or a loan, in that case too, it's very important to know the right value of the property.

So, now we have seen that there can be different reasons for doing valuation of a property. So, let's now start with HOW? i.e. how we do property valuations? What all methods are there to value a property, let's now see that. Some of you might know that I am from Ludhiana, Punjab, so I will be using some examples of my area to tell you about property valuation and how to do that in a real life scenario, and you can do it for your area as well by using similar kind of techniques and methods. So, let's now see that:

As we all know, **Property valuation is the process of determining the value of a piece of real estate.**

There are several methods that can be used to value a property, including:

1. Comparable sales method: This method involves comparing the subject property to similar properties that have recently sold in the same area. The value of the subject property is determined by analyzing the sale prices of the comparable properties, and making adjustments for any differences in size, condition, and other factors. This is the most used method and also called Fair market value method.

2. Income capitalization method: This method is typically used to value income-producing properties such as rental properties and commercial buildings. The value of the property is determined by dividing the net operating income (NOI) by a capitalization rate. This is also called Rent-Yield method in common language.

3. Cost approach: This method estimates the cost to replace the subject property with a similar property, and then subtracts any physical depreciation. This method is typically used for newer properties or properties that have undergone significant renovations.

4. Sales Comparison Approach : This method compares the subject property to similar properties that have recently been sold and are currently on the market. The value of the subject property is determined by analyzing the sale prices of the comparable properties, and making adjustments for any differences in size, condition, and other factors.

5. Residual method: This method is used for property development projects, it estimates the potential income generated by the completed development and deducts all the costs incurred for the development, including land costs, construction costs, and any other costs, to arrive at the value of the property. This is similar to the Land and Building method, which is used for valuing under-construction properties.

6. AVM (Automated Valuation Model) : This method uses a computer program to estimate the value of a property based on data from comparable sales and other data sources.

Apart from these, there maybe more methods to value a property like Market Data Approach (This method involves using market data, such as sales prices and rental rates, to estimate the value of a property. It is based on the principle of supply and demand in the real estate market), or Hybrid Method (Combining two or more of the above methods to arrive at the final value of the property) or what we can say is the choice of method used will depend on the type of property being valued, the intended use of the valuation, and the availability of data.

Additionally, different countries or jurisdictions may have different regulations or standards for property valuation, which may affect the choice of the method used. As for most of the properties, we use the Comparable Sales approach or Fair market value method, for some specific cases, we can use Income Capitalization or Rent-Yield method and for under-construction properties we can use the Residual or Land and Building method. So, which method to use depends on conditions, location, purpose of the valuation and type of the property mostly.

It's important to note that more than one method may be used to value a property, and a professional appraiser will consider all the methods and take the most appropriate approach.

Now, let's discuss all these methods in detail with some examples as well:

1. The comparable sales method,

also known as the market approach, involves comparing the property being valued to similar properties that have recently sold in the same area. The idea is that properties that are similar in terms of size, location, condition, and amenities will have similar values. It is widely used for valuating residential properties. Here's an example of how this method could be used to value a 3 BHK house with some amenities in Panjab Mata Nagar, Ludhiana:

A. Research recent sales of similar properties in the same area. In this case, you would look for other 3 BHK houses with similar amenities that have sold in Panjab Mata Nagar, Ludhiana in the last 6–12 months.

B. Collect data on these comparable properties, including the sale price, size, location, condition, and amenities.

C. Adjust the sale prices of the comparable properties for any differences between them and the property being valued. For example, if the comparable properties have a different number of bathrooms or a different type of flooring, you would adjust the sale prices accordingly.

D. Average the adjusted sale prices of the comparable properties to arrive at an estimated value for the property being valued.

For example, let's say you found three comparable properties that sold in Panjab Mata Nagar, Ludhiana in the last 6 months.

• Property 1: 3 BHK, 1,800 sq ft, with a swimming pool and gym, sold for Rs. 1.2 Crores

- Property 2: 3 BHK, 1,800 sq ft, with a garden and balcony, sold for Rs. 1.1 Crores
- Property 3: 3 BHK, 1,800 sq ft, with a garage and storage room, sold for Rs. 1.15 Crores

After adjusting for the differences in amenities, you might arrive at an estimated value for the property being valued of Rs. 1.15 Crores (average of the adjusted sale prices of the comparable properties).

It is important to note that this is a very much simplified example, and in practice it will require more comparable properties and more adjustments. Also, it is more important to note that the method is based on the assumption that the market conditions remain similar, and the comparable properties are truly similar to the property being valued. So, it's like a fairy tale story which I just told you, right? Because in real life, property valuations are not so easy like the one I just showed you.

But from here, you must have observed one thing, that according to this method, property prices at core, depends on demand and supply. And yes, demand and supply do further depend on so many factors, because of course everyone wants to live in a Tier-1 city where there are more employment opportunities, everyone wants to live in a safe locality, where markets are near, and some amenities are provided. Carpet area, Built-up and Super built-up area are also one of the most important factors. Now, let me now tell you a real life incident where we did property valuation using this method, let's see that:

So, One of my closest friend, Rajveer wanted a 3BHK flat in the Whitefield area, Bangalore in 2019. So the flat she liked, let's call it property A. We first found out if there was any other flat available for sale in that complex or nearby, so we could estimate from that. Now, we found this comparable property, let's say it as property B which was just sold 1–2 months ago. It was a 3BHK in the same apartment. We got the idea of property B's price from the broker who sold it, and similarly you can get the price quote from a nearby broker, and also you can check it online from some websites, i.e., 99 acres, Magic bricks, Housing, Common floor, Makaan, etc. These are 5–6 websites that are very common in India. So, whichever is the most popular website in your area, you can search there about your apartment complex or the surrounding area, whatever the rate of 1,2,3BHK is going on. What you can do, you can also get an idea of the price of raw property and from there you can as well estimate the price of B and A.

So after we found the price of the property B (It was 1 crore), then we calculated it's per square ft. rate. Its built-up area was 1000 square feet. Then after dividing 1 crore with 1000, we got that Rs.10,000 is the rate per square feet. And the property my friend, Rajveer wanted to buy was 1500 square feet. So we multiplied it by 10,000 and got the number 1.5 crores. Now, broker or agent always quote the price 5-10% higher than the actual price, because they leave some scope for negotiations. So, we did negotiations and got a final deal around 145 Lakhs.

Now, this was simple because we got a comparable property (furnished) to compare with the property we wanted to buy, but in case you get the price idea for a raw property, then after this, you will add a premium for a better location and better amenities. Now, it can be a luxury apartment with lots of amenities like a swimming pool, kids' play area, badminton courts, and tennis courts. So, there is a premium for such amenities. Then there are some flats where a lot of work has been done like the modular kitchen is installed, some furniture has been given. So, you will give extra money for these premium factors.

Coming to the location, For location, you must check how far your location is from the city center or CBD, i.e., Central Business District. If we talk about Gurugram, then in Gurugram, the CBD area is the Cybercity, where maximum companies are located, so the surrounding area there is quite expensive. On the other hand, If we see Sohna road, it is roughly 10 Km away from the cyber city. It's a little far, that's why it will be less expensive there. This way, you can get an estimate of the location. The areas around cyber city will be 10-15% expensive, sometimes 25% too. And on Sohna road, you can get a discounting factor and compare it with the area around the cyber city.

Next, you will see the infrastructure, Are there schools nearby? Or Are there hospitals and transportation facilities available? You will see, where there are metros, the rates are a bit high, sometimes 15 or 20-25% higher. Then higher and lower floors also make some difference. If we talk about the top floor, it is generally 10% lower than the rest of the flat. If we talk about Mumbai, then in Mumbai, as the floor increases, the property's price also increases, because of the view, people are ready to pay the extra premium, but this is not the case in Delhi NCR, people prefer lower floors. Therefore, the price of the higher floor decreases. In this way, you can check how much premium you can pay for that property. People also pay an extra premium for park-facing, vastu-compliant properties etc. It can be a 5-10%

premium.

And then if there is furniture, maybe 4–5 years old, you can easily take 40-70% depreciation on that and maybe add only Rs. 5–7 lakhs for a 13–14 lakhs of furniture. Therefore, all this creates a slight difference. Then there is PLC, which is Preferential location charges.

These location charges are really important in many cases, especially if it's a commercial property. Now, for a commercial property, If there is a road-facing property, its price must be very high. If it's three sides open, or it has more frontage, or it is two sides open, then these are premium commanding properties. It can be 50-60% extra in case of a commercial property.

So, this is how you can get an idea of the right value of the property, you want to buy or sell. You can easily deduct 5-10% from the quote you get, and in case you get the idea for a raw property, you can easily give 10-15% premium for location and amenities depending on the factors I discussed above.

So, this is how we do the valuation of a property using Comparable Sales approach.

2. The income capitalization method,

also known as the income approach, is used for income-producing properties such as rental properties or commercial buildings. It involves estimating the income the property will generate and then using that income to estimate the property's value. Here's an example of how this method could be used to value a 3 BHK house in Panjab Mata Nagar, Ludhiana:

A. Estimate the potential rental income for the property. You would need to research the current rental rates for similar properties in the same area, and take into account factors such as size, location, condition, and amenities.

B. Determine the property's operating expenses. These would include expenses such as property taxes, insurance, maintenance and repairs, and management fees.

C. Calculate the property's net operating income (NOI) by subtracting the operating expenses from the potential rental income.

D. Choose an appropriate cap rate, also known as **capitalization rate.** A cap rate is the ratio of the net operating income to the property value. It is used to translate the net operating income into a property value. Cap rates are usually taken from the similar properties in the area.

E. Use the cap rate to calculate the property's value by dividing the NOI by the cap rate.

For example, let's say you estimate the potential rental income for the property to be Rs. 50,000 per month, and the operating expenses are Rs. 20,000 per month. This would result in a net operating income of Rs. 30,000 per month. If you assume a cap rate of 8%, you would calculate the property's value to be Rs. 3.75 Crores (NOI/Cap Rate).

It is important to note that this is a simplified example and in practice it will require more detailed research and calculations. Additionally, the income capitalization method relies on the accuracy of the projected income and expenses, as well as the chosen cap rate. The cap rate is usually taken from similar properties in the area, so it is important to ensure that the property being valued is similar to the comparable properties.

3. The cost approach,

also known as the reproduction or replacement cost method, is a method that estimates the cost of replacing the property with a new one, and then subtracts any depreciation. Here's an example of how this method could be used to value a 3 BHK house in Panjab Mata Nagar, Ludhiana:

A. Determine the cost of reproducing the property. This would involve researching the cost of materials and labor to build a new house with similar size, location, condition, and amenities as the property being valued.

B. Calculate the property's physical depreciation. This would take into account factors such as the age of the property, condition, and any functional obsolescence.

C. Add the reproduction cost and any site value to the calculated physical depreciation to arrive at the property's value.

For example, let's say you determine the cost of reproducing a similar house in the same area to be Rs. 1.5 Crores, and the physical depreciation of the property being valued to be 10% because of its age. If you also assume that the land value is Rs. 50 Lakhs. Then the property value would be Rs. 1.45 Crores (Reproduction cost - Physical Depreciation + Site value).

It is important to note that this is also a simplified example and in practice it will require more detailed research and calculations. Additionally, this method assumes that the property can be replaced with a new one with similar characteristics, which may not always be the case. The cost approach is generally used for special purpose properties or commercial properties, where it is difficult to find similar comparable sales and the income method is not applicable.

4. The residual approach,

also known as the development or land value method, is a method that is used to value land and development opportunities. It is generally used to value properties that are intended for development, such as raw land or properties that are to be demolished and rebuilt. Here's an example of how this method could be used to value a property in Panjab Mata Nagar, Ludhiana:

A. Estimate the gross development value (GDV) of the property. This would involve researching the potential selling prices of similar properties in the area once they are developed.

B. Estimate the costs of developing the property. These costs would include site preparation, construction, professional fees, and any other costs associated with the development of the property.

C. Subtract the estimated development costs from the GDV to determine the residual land value.

For example, let's say you estimate the GDV of a similar property in the same area to be Rs. 2 Crores, and the costs of developing the property to be Rs. 1.5 Crores. The residual land value of the property being valued would be Rs. 50 Lakhs (Gross Development Value - development costs).

It is important to note that this is also a simplified example and in practice it will require more detailed research and calculations. Additionally, the residual approach relies on accurate estimates of the GDV and development costs, as well as the assumption that the property will be developed in a manner consistent with the estimates. This approach might be less commonly used as it is generally used for valuing land and development opportunities and is not applied to finished properties.

5. An automated valuation model (AVM),

is a type of algorithm that uses data from public records and other sources to estimate the value of a property. AVMs are commonly used by financial institutions and real estate companies to quickly and efficiently value properties. Here's an example of how an AVM could be used to value a property in Panjab Mata Nagar, Ludhiana:

A. Collect data about the property being valued, such as the address, size, number of rooms, and other features.

B. Gather data from public records and other sources, such as recent sales of similar properties in the area, property tax assessments, and demographic information.

C. Use the collected data to train an algorithm or model that can estimate the value of the property being valued. The algorithm will take into account various factors such as location, size, age, condition, and amenities of the property and comparable properties.

D. Use the trained model to estimate the value of the property being valued.

It is important to note that AVMs rely on the availability and accuracy of the data used to train the model. Additionally, the accuracy of the AVM's estimate may vary depending on the specific model and the data inputs. AVMs are not a substitute for a professional property valuation, especially for properties that are unique or for properties that are in an area where data is scarce. AVMs are commonly used for mass appraisal and for providing an estimate for properties for which a professional property valuation would be too expensive or time-consuming.

6. The hybrid method,

combines two or more of the previously discussed methods (market, income, cost) to arrive at the property's value. The idea is that by using multiple methods, the valuer can arrive at a more accurate estimate of the property's value by accounting for the strengths and limitations of each individual method. Here's an example of how the hybrid method could be used to value a property in Panjab Mata Nagar, Ludhiana:

A. Research recent sales of similar properties in the same area using the comparable sales method.

B. Estimate the potential rental income for the property and determine the property's operating expenses using the income capitalization method.

C. Determine the cost of reproducing the property and calculate the property's physical depreciation using the cost approach.

D. Compare the values obtained from each method and consider the strengths and limitations of each method to arrive at a final value for the property.

For example, let's say the comparable sales method estimate the value of the property to be Rs. 1.15 Crores, the income capitalization method estimate the value to be Rs. 3.75 Crores and the cost approach estimate the value to be Rs. 1.45 Crores. The valuer would take into account the specific circumstances of the property, such as its location, condition, and intended use, as well as the strengths and limitations of each method to arrive at a final value for the property. The final value could be a weighted average of all the three methods, or it could be one of the value obtained from the methods, depending on the valuer's judgement and the specific circumstances of the property.

It is important to note that this is also a much simplified example and in practice, it will require more detailed research and calculations. Additionally, the hybrid method relies on the accuracy of the data used in each method and the valuer's judgement in deciding how to combine the results. The Hybrid method is useful when the property has unique characteristics, and it is difficult to estimate its value using a single method.

So, these are some of the methods we can use for valuing a property. And these examples can be a good starting point for you in calculating the right value of a property. For an exercise purpose, try to calculate the value of your own home or flat or if you are a shop-owner, the right price of your shop is? Try to find out the answer to these fun exercises. It will help you clear your concepts regarding property valuations.

CHAPTER THREE

Property Documentation

This section is specially for buyers or potential buyers of real estate (mainly residential and commercial properties). Before buying a real estate property in India, it is important to review and verify the following documents because there are many possible frauds, which can happen, if documents are not properly checked. So, you should always see these documents:

1. Title Deed or Sale Deed:

This document proves the legal ownership of the property. This is the most important document. A title deed contains important information about the property such as the legal description of the property, the names of the current and previous owners, and any encumbrances or legal disputes associated with the property. It is crucial to review and verify the title deed before purchasing a property to ensure that there are no issues with the property's ownership. When reviewing the title deed, it is important to check for the following:

A. The names of the current and previous owners: Make sure that the names on the title deed match the names of the seller and that there are no outstanding claims on the property. Also check here the **Channel document**, which will be having the names of all previous owners.

B. Encumbrances: An encumbrance is a legal claim on a property, such as a mortgage or lien. Check the title deed for any encumbrances to ensure that they have been cleared before the sale.

C. Legal disputes: Check for any legal disputes associated with the property, such as pending lawsuits or unresolved disputes with neighbors.

D. Property description: Make sure that the legal description of the property on the title deed matches the physical property and that there are no discrepancies.

2. Encumbrance Certificate (EC):

This document certifies that the property is free from any financial liabilities or legal disputes. It is issued by the office of the Sub-Registrar where the property is registered, and it contains information about the property such as the owner's name, the property's location, and the legal transactions that have taken place on the property, such as mortgages, liens, or court cases. The EC is usually valid for a period of 30 days from the date of issue, and it is considered an important document to check before purchasing a property. It serves as proof that the property has no outstanding debts or legal issues that could be passed on to the new owner. It's important to note that checking the EC is not only for the benefit of the buyer but also for the seller as well, as it protects the seller from any future legal disputes that may arise from any undisclosed liabilities of the property.

3. Building Plan Approval and Completion Certificate:

A Building Plan Approval is a document that certifies that the construction plans for a property have been reviewed and approved by the local municipal corporation or other relevant authorities. It is issued after the plans have been submitted and reviewed, and it confirms that the construction will comply with local building codes and regulations. A Building Completion Certificate, on the other hand, is a document that certifies that the property constructed, is in accordance with the approved building plans and that it is fit for occupation. It is issued after an inspection of the completed construction by the local authorities. It is mandatory for the builder to obtain these certificates from the local authorities before selling the property, and it's important for a buyer to check these documents before purchasing a property. These documents ensure that the property has been constructed as per the approved building plan and is safe for living.

4. Tax Paid Receipts:

This document proves that all taxes on the property have been paid up to date.

5. NOC from Housing Society or Apartment Owners Association:

If the property is in a housing society or apartment complex, an NOC from the society or association is required. A No Objection Certificate (NOC) is a document that certifies that there are no objections or legal hurdles that would prevent a particular action from taking place. In the context of real estate, an NOC is typically required from a housing society or apartment owners association when a property is located within the society or association's jurisdiction. The NOC from the society or association is a proof that all the dues and charges, such as maintenance charges, have been cleared by the seller, and that there are no pending disputes or complaints against the property. It also confirms that the society or association has no objections to the transfer of ownership of the property. The NOC is typically issued by the Secretary of the society or association, and it should include information such as the name of the seller, the property's location, and the date on which the NOC was issued. It's important to note that the NOC requirement may vary depending on the location and type of property you're looking to purchase.

Now, these were some documents which were completely necessary to check before buying any real estate or property in India and these should be available for almost all kinds of properties in India, but except these, there are some more documents, which, depends on type, location etc. of the property and if needed (in case it is), you can check those as well. The following documents are not very much necessary and won't be available for every kind of property, but in some cases, these documents, as well, will be very necessary to check before buying that property. These are:

Conversion Certificate (if applicable): This document is required if the property has been converted from agricultural land to non-agricultural land,

Lease Deed (if applicable): This document is required if the property is on leasehold land,

Possession Letter (if applicable): This document confirms that the seller has possession of the property and is authorized to sell it,

Khata or Property Tax Receipt (if applicable): This document proves that the property is registered with the local municipal corporation and tax has been paid,

Power of Attorney (if applicable): If the property is being purchased through a power of attorney, the original copy of the power of attorney is required,

The Car Allotment Letter (In case of flats), this provides parking space for your car, **NOCs** from various other departments as well is required in some cases, and then there is,

Mutation document (Namankaran), process of changing the name in government records, it is done when a property is sold from A to B, here, property is converted from A to B's name in this document. After purchasing the property, you must register this in government records.

These are all the documents, which can be required to sell a property, or you should see and check these documents before buying a property. It is always recommended to take the help of a legal expert (lawyer) to verify these documents before finalizing the purchase, as these requirements may vary depending on the location and type of property you are looking to purchase.

Now, let's see the process of property registration in India. It is a legal process that involves several steps, including:

1. Obtaining the original sale or gift deed - This is the first step in the registration process and involves obtaining the original sale or gift deed from the seller or giver. The deed should be stamped and registered with the appropriate authority.

2. Paying stamp duty - This is the second step and involves paying stamp duty on the value of the property. The stamp duty is calculated based on the value of the property and varies from state to state.

3. Filing the registration application - The next step is to file the registration application with the sub-registrar office in the jurisdiction where the property is located. The application should be accompanied by the original sale or gift deed, as well as a copy of the PAN card and Aadhaar card of the buyer and seller.

4. Verification of documents - The sub-registrar will verify the documents and conduct a site inspection to ensure that the property is not under dispute and that all the necessary taxes and fees have been paid.

5. Payment of registration fee - After the documents are verified, the registration fee must be paid. The fee is calculated based on the value of the property and varies from state to state.

6. Execution of the deed - Once the registration fee is paid, the registration deed is executed in the presence of the buyer and seller, and two witnesses.

7. Issuance of the registration certificate - After the registration deed is executed, the sub-registrar will issue the registration certificate, which serves as proof of ownership of the property.

It's important to note that the process of property registration may vary from state to state, and it's best to consult a lawyer or a property expert for guidance in the process.

Frauds in Real Estate Market and How to Protect Yourself:

There are several potential frauds that can occur in the Indian real estate market. Some of the most common ones include:

1. Property fraud: This occurs when a fraudster poses as the owner of a property and sells it to an unsuspecting buyer. The buyer may not realize that the property is not legally owned by the seller until it is too late.

2. Document fraud: This occurs when fraudsters create fake or forged documents such as title deeds, encumbrance certificates, and building plans to trick buyers into purchasing a property.

3. Land scams: This occurs when fraudsters sell land that is not legally owned by them or sell land that is reserved for specific purposes, such as agriculture or government use.

4. Unapproved colonies: Some fraudsters may sell plots in unapproved colonies or layouts, these colonies are not legal and may not have proper infrastructure, amenities and may not be eligible for government schemes.

In order to protect yourself from these frauds, it's important to take the following precautions:

1. Verify documents: Always verify the authenticity of documents such as title deeds, encumbrance certificates, and building plans before purchasing a property.

2. Conduct a property search: Check the property's land records and ensure that the property is not in a disputed area or does not have any encumbrances.

3. Hire a lawyer: It is always recommended to hire a lawyer who specializes in real estate to review the documents and advise you on the legal aspects of the property.

4. Check for approvals: Verify that the building plans have been approved by the local authority and that the property is located in an approved colony or layout.

5. Be suspicious of too-good-to-be-true deals: Be cautious of deals that seem too good to be true or if the price is significantly lower than the market rate.

6. Avoid cash transactions: Avoid cash transactions and always use cheques or electronic transfer to make payments.

It is always recommended to be cautious and take the necessary steps to protect yourself from real estate frauds. Furthermore, it's always a good idea to consult a lawyer or the local authorities for proper guidance.

CHAPTER FOUR

How to Become a Real Estate Millionaire Investor

You must have seen that 80-90% of the world's millionaires are millionaires because they have worked in the real estate sector. So, Real Estate has a capacity to make someone a millionaire if he/she follows the right path, as Real Estate gives you so many opportunities to earn so much money. If you have a CA friend, or if you run a business, you would be knowing that we say "Land never depreciates." Now, why is that even true? Because, we studied in the valuations chapter, that property prices are based on demand and supply. And, supply of land on Earth is limited, demand is continuously increasing and that's why, land should always appreciate in value. But this is just a trailer, real money which these millionaires made, is not only from appreciation, that will constitute maximum only 10-15% of their incomes. Real money is made by flipping, yes, **Flipping the Real Estate**. Let's deep dive into that:

Now, mostly there are these five ways through which people become millionaires in Real Estate:

1. Instant Equity or Buying at a Discount:

The instant equity or buying at a discount strategy in real estate investing refers to the practice of purchasing a property for less than its market value, with the goal of quickly reselling it for a profit or maybe do some changes in it and then flip it for higher profits. We will study about the second one in more detail in 3rd way. This can be achieved through a variety of methods, such as negotiating with the seller, finding properties that are undervalued due to repairs needed, or buying foreclosed or distressed properties i.e. sometimes the seller have an emergency to sell (He wanted to start a business, or maybe for some reasons, he needs urgent cash) he/she wants to get money as soon as possible, so that opens door for you for good negotiations, and definitely you can get a good discount here. Mostly, you will need to find these kinds of properties, which only your network with brokers or agents can help you here, so networking is the key in Real Estate Industry.

The basic idea behind the strategy is that a property can be purchased at a lower price, and then quickly sold for a higher price. The difference between the purchase price and the sales price is the "instant equity" that is created. For example, if a property is purchased for $100,000 and is subsequently sold for $120,000, the investor has created $20,000 in instant equity. This profit can be used to purchase additional properties or to invest in other ventures.

It's important to note that this strategy requires a good understanding of the real estate market, and the ability to identify properties that are undervalued. Additionally, it also requires access to capital, and the ability to move quickly when an opportunity arises. Furthermore, it's important to consider all the costs involved in the transaction, such as repairs, renovation, closing costs and agent fees, to have a clear understanding of the actual profit made from the transaction.

In summary, the "instant equity" or "buying at a discount" strategy in real estate investing refers to the practice of purchasing a property for less than its market value with the goal of quickly reselling it for a profit by creating instant equity. It requires good market knowledge, quick decision-making and available capital.

2. More cash inflows than outflows:

One thing an investor in a property must understand is that the particular property in which you are investing, must generate positive cashflows, basically NPV greater than 0 (Net Present Value). Here, your cash inflows will be rent, which is coming to you every month and your outflows will be some expenses, maybe property taxes, insurance, any repairment, EMIs or anything. So, you must ensure that the cash you will be receiving (cash inflows i.e. Rent) should be greater than the expenses (cash outflows) and the property must generate some positive cashflows. Mostly, in India, in normal places, rent is 3-4% and NPV is 2-3% of the property price and in case of a commercial property or a PG, at a good location, it maybe rises up to 5-7% or in some extreme cases, to 10% as well. So, this is very necessary.

3. *Forced Appreciation:*

Now, this is a method to increase property's value by magic. It actually does wonders. Suppose you bought a property at Rs. 35 lakhs, and you make some repairs there, some furnishing, paint, cleaning etc. and then you kind of transform that home with 4 rooms into a PG with 4 different rooms, so where you would be renting this to one family and take rent maybe Rs. 15,000/- per month, now, there, you can rent it to four students and take rent Rs. 5000/- from each student per month, which sums up to Rs. 20,000/- per month. This is a very much simplified example, there might be some other expenses as well, and it will depend on many other factors as well. So, this is how we do forced appreciation.

What it means is, we buy a property, we transform it, maybe we add one more bedroom there, one bathroom, improve kitchen, lawn etc. just to increase its value on a multiple. Suppose you bought a property for Rs. 50 lakhs and transforming it (Doing paint etc.) costs you Rs. 15 lakhs, Now, if you did that correctly, if you did the required and correct (right) changes, then there is a possibility that this property might now be sold for Rs. 80–85 lakhs in 2–3 months, depending on that area. But to use this method, you need to be observant that what is happening in outside world, where the demand is going, what is requirements nowadays and most importantly what is happening in property sector in this specific area. Then, you can make good money with this forced appreciation method.

4. *Leverage:*

This is the most important and most useful money-making method in Real Estate industry. Leverage refers to using borrowed money to increase the potential return on an investment. In the context of real estate, leverage can be used to purchase property with a smaller amount of cash, while borrowing the remaining amount.

For example, if an investor wants to purchase a $100,000 property, they may put down a 20% down payment of $20,000 and borrow the remaining $80,000 from a lender. The investor can then use the property to generate income through renting or flipping. The return on investment (ROI) can be much higher than if the investor had paid for the entire property in cash, as the investor is only using $20,000 of their own money. However, leverage also increases the risk because if the property doesn't generate enough income to cover the mortgage payments, the investor may default on the loan and lose the property.

Now, Suppose, if you have $100,000/- and you go to buy a property of $100,000/- and there you will be able to buy only one property, and suppose in 5 years, it appreciates to $500,000/-, here you will make a profit of $400,000 and suppose if you make the right use of leverage, and you bought these properties with the down payment of 20% and other 80% via a loan and then, you will be able to buy five such properties, and they will appreciate to $500,000*5= $2,500,000/- and your profit is exponentially increased, but yes, there are some expenses in this case, that will be your EMIs, for that you have to ensure that properties you are buying will definitely generate positive cashflows or more cash inflows will be there than outflows so that you can pay for your EMIs. And again, this was a very simple example, in reality, the conditions will be much competitive and different, With experience, you can easily learn how to handle these kinds of situations. But yes, Leverage really do wonders.

5. Appreciation (Over time):

In real estate, appreciation refers to an increase in the value of a property over time. This increase in value can be caused by a variety of factors, such as improvements made to the property, changes in the local real estate market, or simply the passage of time. Here, in this case, we are talking about the increase in property prices with time i.e. If a property at a good location with good other factors is priced today at Rs. 1 crore, then it will definitely appreciate and give good returns with time. It's important to note here that real estate is a less risky investment than equity, so in general, if we see, appreciation of property prices is around 8-10% or at good locations, 10-12% over time, but some people actually generate much more money than this number in real estate. Appreciation can be a significant benefit to real estate investors, as it can lead to significant returns on their investment over time.

This strategy is known as Fix and Flip strategy, of course in reality when I did this I used some more strategies with this in a mixture (Hybrid strategy), which we just discussed and as you can see, all these five factors Buying at a discount, Positive NPV, Forced appreciation, leverage and appreciation over time are additive in nature, that means if one or two of them are not even working, then also you can make a good money because your total return consist of the sum of returns you get from each factor i.e. Suppose you were not able to get the property at a discount, but then you made some good repairs and actually sold that at a very high price, then as well, you are making a good return, just because you are not able to perform good at one factor does not mean you will not get good return, another example would be, Suppose property prices in that area did not appreciate for 2–3 years, where you made this property investment, but because you bought it at a discount, that's why, you are still sitting on a good return, This is why, this is my personal favorite strategy and I love to do this with properties always.

Now, this was one strategy that I discussed in detail above, there are many more other strategies which you can use to make a million dollars or more in real estate industry.

So for that you need to decide your niche and strategy first. Let me give you some ideas:

Your Niche can be **Residential real estate** (Single-family homes, townhouses, and condominiums),

Commercial real estate (Office buildings, retail spaces, warehouses, and other properties used for business purposes),

Industrial real estate (Factories, warehouses, and other properties used for manufacturing and distribution),

Hospitality real estate (Hotels, motels, resorts, and other properties used for lodging and vacation rentals),

Multifamily real estate (Apartment buildings, duplexes, triplexes, and other properties with multiple units),

Land (Undeveloped land, farmland, and lots for future development),

Special-purpose real estate (Properties used for specific purposes such as self-storage, senior housing, student housing, medical office),

International real estate (Properties located outside the India) etc.

And you can apply these various strategies:

1. Buy and Hold Strategy:

The buy and hold strategy in real estate refers to buying a property with the intention of holding onto it for a long period of time, typically several years or more. The goal of this strategy is to generate income through rental income and/or appreciation of the property's value.

For example, an investor may purchase a multi-unit rental property with the intention of renting out the units and holding onto the property for a number of years. As the property increases in value and the investor continues to collect rental income, they may eventually sell the property for a profit. Another example could be, an investor buys a property in an upcoming area, where the property prices are low, and the demand is high. This investor plans to hold on to the property for several years until the area develops and the property value increases. They may then sell the property for a higher price, earning a profit.

It's important to note that the buy and hold strategy is not suitable for short-term investments or for those who want to flip properties quickly, as it requires a long-term commitment and a significant amount of capital upfront.

2. Fix-and-Flipping Strategy:

This is the one which we just discussed above, for explaining to you the above 5 terms in starting of this chapter, we just used this method because this is my personal favorite method, and I love doing this to properties. The fix-and-flip strategy in real estate refers to buying a property that is in need of repairs or renovations, fixing it up, and then reselling it for a profit. The goal of this strategy is to quickly buy and sell properties in order to make a profit. This strategy is more suitable for short-term investments and requires less capital upfront than the buy-and-hold strategy.

For example, an investor may find a property that is in need of repairs or renovations, such as a fixer-upper. They will then purchase the property, make the necessary repairs and improvements, and resell the property for a higher price. The investor's goal is to complete the repairs and resell the property as quickly as possible, ideally within a few months, in order to maximize the profit margin. Another example could be, an investor buys a property at auction at a low price, and finds out that the property is in a good location but needs some repairs. The investor then makes the necessary repairs and improvements and lists the property for sale at a higher price. The investor's goal is to make a profit on the sale of the property.

It's important to note that fix-and-flipping requires a significant amount of knowledge and experience in real estate, as well as a good understanding of the market and the ability to accurately estimate repair costs and potential resale value.

3. Wholesaling Strategy:

The wholesaling strategy in real estate refers to the process of finding and contracting to buy a property at a low price, and then quickly reselling the contract to another buyer, usually an investor, at a higher price. Wholesaling does not involve taking ownership of the property, and the goal is to make a profit from the difference between the purchase price and the resale price. For example, an investor may find a property that is being sold at a significant discount, perhaps due to a motivated seller or a property that needs repairs. The investor would then enter into a purchase contract with the seller and then quickly resell the contract to another investor at a higher price. The investor who wholesales the property does not take ownership of the property, and the final buyer will be the one who takes the ownership and makes the necessary repairs and improvements. Another example could be, an investor finds a property that is being sold by an estate sale or public auction at a low price, the investor then quickly contracts the property and assigns the contract to another investor for a higher price.

It's important to note that wholesaling requires a significant amount of knowledge and experience in real estate, as well as a good understanding of the market and the ability to quickly find and contract properties at a low price. Additionally, it's important to know the laws and regulations in your area, as wholesaling is not legal in all states and also may require certain licenses.

4. Development Strategy:

The development strategy in real estate refers to the process of acquiring land or existing properties and then improving them by adding new buildings or infrastructure, such as by building new homes, apartments, or commercial spaces. The goal of this strategy is to increase the value of the property by developing it into a more valuable asset, which can then be sold or leased for a profit. For example, an investor may acquire a piece of land in a rapidly growing area and develop it into a residential community. The investor would then build new homes or apartments on the land and sell or rent them for a profit. Another example could be, an investor acquires a run-down commercial building in a prime location and develops it into a mixed-use property with retail and office spaces. The investor would then lease the space to tenants and generate rental income from the property.

It's important to note that development strategy requires a significant amount of capital and expertise in construction, planning, and design, as well as a good understanding of the market and the ability to identify and capitalize on opportunities for development. Additionally, it's also important to be aware of laws, regulations and zoning laws in your area.

5. Turnkey Strategy:

The turnkey strategy in real estate refers to buying a property that is already generating rental income, and is ready for immediate occupancy. The goal of this strategy is to generate passive income through rental income, without the need for significant renovations or repairs. This strategy is typically used by investors who are looking for a lower-maintenance and more hands-off approach to real estate investing.

For example, an investor may purchase a single-family home that is already being rented out to tenants, and is fully managed by a property management company. The investor can start earning rental income right away, without the need to make any repairs or improvements. Another example could be, an investor buys a multi-unit apartment building that is already fully occupied by tenants and is also managed by a professional property management company. The investor can start earning rental income from the day of purchase, without the need to worry about finding tenants or managing the property.

It's important to note that turnkey properties are typically more expensive than properties that need repairs or renovations, but they also offer a less risky and lower-maintenance option for investors looking for a more passive real estate investment. Additionally, it's important to do your due diligence and research the property, the area, and the property management company, as well as the current and potential rental income and expenses, to ensure that the investment is profitable.

6. BRRRR Strategy:

The BRRRR strategy in real estate stands for "Buy, Rehab, Rent, Refinance, Repeat", is a real estate investment strategy that focuses on buying distressed or undervalued properties, rehabilitating them, renting them out, and then refinancing the property to take out the initial investment, so that the investor can repeat the process with another property. The goal of this strategy is to generate cash flow and build wealth through the acquisition and improvement of rental properties.

For example, an investor may find a property that is in need of repairs, but is located in a desirable rental area. They would then buy the property, make the necessary repairs and improvements, and rent it out. Once the property is generating rental income, the investor would then refinance the property, taking out the initial investment and leaving a portion of the rental income as cash flow. They can then repeat the process with another property.

Another example could be, an investor buys a property, with the intention of fixing it up, renting it out and then refinancing it to take out the initial investment and use the cash to buy another property, the investor can repeat this process several times, leveraging the equity built in each property to acquire more properties, thus creating a portfolio of rental properties.

It's important to note that BRRRR strategy requires a significant amount of knowledge and experience in real estate, as well as a good understanding of the market, and the ability to accurately estimate repair costs and potential resale value. Additionally, it also requires a good credit score and the ability to qualify for refinancing.

7. House Hacking Strategy:

The house hacking strategy in real estate refers to the process of purchasing a multi-unit property, such as a duplex, triplex, or fourplex, and living in one unit while renting out the other units to generate rental income. The goal of this strategy is to generate cash flow and reduce housing costs by offsetting the cost of the mortgage with rental income.

For example, an investor may purchase a duplex and live in one unit while renting out the other unit. The rental income from the second unit would then be used to offset the cost of the mortgage, reducing the investor's housing expenses.

Another example could be, an investor buys a triplex and lives in one unit, rents out the other two units. The rental income from the other two units will be used to offset the cost of the mortgage, and also generate a positive cash flow.

It's important to note that house hacking strategy can be a great way to get started in real estate investing, as it allows an investor to live in the property and learn about the responsibilities of being a landlord while also generating rental income. Additionally, it's important to be aware of the laws and regulations in your area, as well as the tax implications of renting out a portion of your primary residence.

8. *Student Rentals Strategy:*

The student rental strategy in real estate refers to the process of purchasing properties in areas with a high concentration of students, such as college towns, and renting them out to students as a form of investment. This strategy is based on the idea that college towns tend to have high demand for rental properties, as students are consistently in need of housing during the academic year. For example, an investor may purchase a multi-unit apartment building near a college campus, and rent out the units to students. The investor can then charge a premium for rent, due to the high demand for housing near the campus. Another example could be, an investor buys a single-family home in a college town and rents it out to students as a shared accommodation, this way the investor can charge a higher rent per room, and also get a higher occupancy rate.

It's important to note that the student rental strategy can be a profitable investment as long as there's a consistent demand for student housing in the area, but it's also important to be aware of the laws and regulations in your area, as well as the potential for vacancy during the summer months, when students are not in school. Additionally, it's important to be aware of the tax implications of renting out a property and also to have a proper screening process for your tenants.

9. *Vacation Rentals Strategy:*

The vacation rental strategy in real estate refers to the process of purchasing properties in areas with high tourist demand, such as beach towns or ski resorts, and renting them out as short-term rentals for vacationers. This strategy is based on the idea that vacationers are willing to pay a premium for short-term rental properties in desirable locations.

For example, an investor may purchase a beachfront condo and rent it out as a vacation rental. The investor can then charge a premium for rent, due to the high demand for beachfront properties and the desirable location.

Another example could be, an investor buys a ski chalet in a popular ski resort, and rents it out to vacationers during the ski season. The investor can charge a premium for rent due to the high demand for ski accommodation during the winter season.

It's important to note that the vacation rental strategy can be a profitable investment as long as there's a consistent demand for vacation rentals in the area, but it's also important to be aware of the laws and regulations in your area, as well as the competition in the market. Additionally, it's important to be aware of the tax implications of renting out a property and also to have a proper management plan in place to handle bookings, cleaning, maintenance and customer service.

There are many more strategies which people use to make money in Real estate, but these were some of the main strategies that pulls out the greatest money and most used in the industry.

Now, you might have one question that, "Gurcharan, you know, we are beginners, right? So how to get started with zero money and how to get into all of this? Ok, ok, I can understand you and I will answer everything one by one. Let's start our discussion with how to enter the real estate market and apply these strategies with 0 money or zero money down, let's see that now:

Applying these strategies with zero money down:

So, for that, you need to understand one key thing, that zero money does not mean that you can buy a real estate with zero money, it means that money does not come from you. I.e. you are investing your zero rupees. Of course, we need to finance the money. From where, we will see that in detail in this section. Let's begin:

So, I suppose you have Rs. 0 today, but you really want to get into this and want to become a real estate millionaire, so what you would do, is, you will probably look for investors who will finance the money for you to buy the properties and apply these strategies. Now, where will you get these investors. Let's talk about that. So, here comes your negotiation, communication and convincing skills. You need to make your network, you can do it via LinkedIn, by going to some events where you can meet

Real Estate Investors, you can join some clubs which have these high net-worth individuals. Watching Shark Tank? It's probably like that, you need to find the investors and convince them who will bet on you, this is the most important and difficult step in our journey, but you have to make your network strong, and you need to build that trust factor.

Let me tell you a story, so, I was working with a builder (let's give it a name, say ABC), basically I was handling all day-to-day operations, and I was the manager at ABC Builders, now, one day, a 19-20 year old boy comes to my office, and he says "Sir, the buildings you are constructing here (our site was near Zirakpur, Punjab) I am able to sell 25+ flats from your building within next 30–60 days, but I need 10-15% discount + 2% fees (From your marketing expenses budget), and I will take money from you after I sell these flats", I said "How can you sell these numbers of flats in pre-launch, it is not possible for you", then he handed over a card to me and said "Sir, this is a Real Estate Investors Club, I am a part of it and I have these persons in my network, and they believe in my capabilities, that's why they will invest their money on the properties I say". So, the point here to note is trust, **TRUST** is the most important factor which will differentiate you from others in the eyes of your investor.

Suppose, you try all these networking options, LinkedIn, via mails, offline events, and you find some investors, you then explain to them your strategies, that this is how you will be fixing and flipping the property, or any other strategy, and then it's your responsibility to find projects/properties where you can apply these strategies. And there your connections with brokers will help you a lot, so, you find suitable projects, you find investors, then you convince them that this is the project, this is what I am going to do, and this is how much return you can expect from this, so mostly, it will be a 50-50 partnership, if you are okayish negotiator, otherwise it depends on you and your soft-skills. So, the investor will be putting in all the 100% money, and you will be putting in your 100% effort and sweat, and then at the end of the project, you both will be getting your profit shares, and this is how you can start. Sometimes, you will get a chance to do Refinance the project in between, so you can take advantage of that as well.

This is how, you will start, you will do one project, one more and then one more and then your investor will have a firm believe in you and trust compounds over time, so he will be investing in you and this is how your name will be made in industry, then you will have a plenty of investors always to finance the property. It is only difficult in starting, when you apply this 1–2 times, then it will become easy and easy for you. But for that you need to start, you have to get out of your comfort zone and try to make your first deal.

But, I know, still many of you will not be believing this story, you will be saying, okay, I will do all this, but in reality, it will be very difficult to make good connections with investors and brokers because this industry is not very easy, there is a cut-throat competition in this industry, there are many big players, smart people in this industry and for you as a single and small entity, it is so easy for them to crush you and investors and brokers can easily make their own deals, with removing you from deal. This will make them more profit and real estate industry, it has big money, but then it has some of the smartest minds of the Earth, I believe, so you have to enter into this room with a lot of passion and hunger in you otherwise there will be no entry in this industry. I believe Real Estate is one of the most competitive industries, but yes, everything is possible, after telling you this hard reality, let me tell you one more reality that how I entered this market, and how I am surviving here and at a good place:

So, I followed this formula to enter into this industry:

I found a Big Real Estate Builder-Broker in my city, Ludhiana and I went to him and asked "Sir, Can I work under you for experience? I really want to learn this sector, I am ready to work for free!", The first one had some issues, he already had a good number of staff, so he did not hire me, but he gave some valuable insights and tips to me and wished me all the very best, and it really boosted my confidence, I then went to the 2nd big name in my city, and there I asked same, and this time, he hired me, and he was paying me according to the industry standards at that time. So, I worked there for 5–6 months and I got an amazing experience there, I made brilliant connections with some builders and investors as well, and then I started my own venture in this space.

This is how I entered this market, and you can as well, but this is not the only way. You can make your own ways as well. This is up to you and I know, you will definitely find some more creative ways to enter into real estate industry.

And let me write an actionable plan in steps, in front of you, so that you can choose what you want to become and how you can do that.

The real estate sector offers a wide range of career opportunities for you.

These are some examples of the various roles and occupations within the industry, which you can choose:

1. Real Estate Agent/Broker: These professionals help buyers and sellers navigate the process of buying and selling property. They typically work for a real estate agency or as independent contractors.

2. Property Manager: These professionals are responsible for managing rental properties, including finding tenants, collecting rent, and handling maintenance and repairs.

3. Real Estate Developer: Developers are responsible for the construction of new properties, including residential and commercial buildings.

4. Real Estate Appraiser: Appraisers determine the value of properties for a variety of purposes, such as mortgages, property tax assessments, and insurance.

5. Real Estate Investment Trust (REIT) Manager: REIT managers are responsible for the management of a REIT, which is a publicly traded company that owns and operates income-producing real estate.

6. Real Estate Financier: Real estate financiers provide funding for real estate projects through various financial instruments like mortgages, bonds, and loans.

7. Real Estate Consultant: Real estate consultants help clients identify and evaluate potential real estate investments, and provide advice on various aspects of the industry.

8. Real Estate Lawyer: Real estate lawyers specialize in legal issues related to the buying, selling, and leasing of properties.

9. Real Estate Architect: Architects design buildings and manage construction projects.

These are just a few examples of the many different roles and occupations within the real estate industry. With the wide range of opportunities, you can choose the role that aligns with your skills, interests and qualifications.

Now, for becoming a Real Estate Developer or Builder, you can follow these steps:

1. Get educated: To become a real estate builder, you need to have a good understanding of the construction process, building codes, and regulations. Consider getting a degree in construction management or a related field.

2. Gather experience: Gain experience in the construction industry through internships, apprenticeships, or working in a related field. This will give you valuable skills and knowledge that will be useful when you start building your own properties.

3. Develop a business plan: Before you start building, you need to have a clear plan in place. This should include your goals, target market, and budget.

4. Obtain funding: Building real estate requires a significant amount of capital. Look for investors, loans, or grants to fund your projects.

5. Obtain necessary licenses and permits: Make sure you have all the necessary licenses and permits to legally build in your area.

6. Build your first project: Start with a small project and work your way up. This will give you the experience and confidence you need to take on bigger projects in the future.

7. Network and market your business: Network with other builders, real estate agents, and potential clients. Use social media, online directories, and other marketing tools to promote your business.

8. Continuously improve and adapt: Stay informed about new trends and technologies in the construction industry and adapt your business accordingly. Continuously improve your skills and knowledge to stay competitive in the market.

And then, mostly, for becoming any other stakeholder in real estate i.e. if you choose any other occupation than builder, then you mainly have to go through these steps to become a successful professional in the real estate industry:

1. Gain knowledge of the real estate market: Familiarize yourself with the current market conditions and trends, including property prices, demand for different types of properties, and government regulations affecting the industry.

2. Obtain a professional qualification: Many roles in the real estate industry require a professional qualification, such as a Real Estate Broker's license or a Property Manager's license. These qualifications can typically be obtained through a combination of education and practical experience.

3. Build a network: Real estate is a people-oriented industry, and having a good network of contacts can be helpful in building a successful career. Attend industry events, join professional associations, and make connections with other professionals in the field.

4. Get hands-on experience: Consider interning or working for a real estate agency or developer to gain practical experience and learn about the day-to-day operations of the industry.

5. Learn about finance and economics: Real estate is closely tied to the broader economy, and understanding how economic conditions can affect the industry can be helpful in making informed decisions.

6. Develop good communication and negotiation skills: In real estate, being able to communicate effectively and negotiate successfully with clients, buyers, and sellers is essential.

7. Continuously keep updating your knowledge: Real estate industry is a dynamic one, stay updated with the latest market trends, government regulations and technologies to stay relevant.

8. Understand the legal aspect: Real estate transactions have a lot of legalities, understanding the legal aspects of buying, selling, leasing and renting property can help you navigate the complexities of the industry.

By following these tips, and focusing on areas of study that are relevant to the specific role you are interested in, you can increase your chances of success in the real estate industry.

Now, at the end of this chapter I would advise you to read about some strategies of some **Real Estate Tycoons,** like in India, there are **Rajiv Singh, Vikas Oberoi, Mangal Prabhat Lodha, Jitendra Virwani** etc. who made big fortunes in real estate sector, so do read about them, what they did, how they did it and relate it with how you can do it as well. In bonus, let me tell you some common strategies that real estate tycoons use to achieve success in the industry.

1. Identifying profitable markets: Successful real estate tycoons often have a deep understanding of the real estate market and are able to identify profitable markets and opportunities before others do.

2. Networking: Building a strong network of contacts in the industry, such as architects, engineers, contractors, and investors, can be crucial to securing funding and getting projects off the ground.

3. Long-term vision: Real estate tycoons often have a long-term vision and are able to identify opportunities that may not be immediately obvious. They are willing to take risks and invest in properties or markets that may not be popular at the time, but have potential for future growth.

4. Financing: Real estate tycoons typically have access to large amounts of capital, which allows them to invest in multiple properties at once and take advantage of economies of scale.

5. Strategic partnerships: Real estate tycoons often form strategic partnerships with other companies or individuals in the industry to access capital, expertise, and other resources.

6. Strong negotiation skills: Real estate tycoons are often skilled negotiators, able to secure favorable deals on properties and financing.

7. Continual learning: Real estate tycoons are often lifelong learners, constantly seeking out new information and staying current on industry trends, technologies and regulations.

In summary, becoming a real estate tycoon requires a combination of strategic thinking, market knowledge, networking, financing, strategic partnerships, strong negotiation skills, and continual learning.

So, In **conclusion**, Becoming a real estate millionaire in India is a challenging but achievable goal. There are several strategies and tactics that can be employed to build wealth through real estate investments in India.

First, it's important to understand the Indian real estate market. India has a rapidly growing population, and as such, the demand for housing is high. Additionally, the Indian economy is growing quickly, which is leading to an increase in disposable income for many Indians. This means that there is a growing market for both affordable and luxury housing.

One strategy for becoming a real estate millionaire in India is to invest in property at a young age. This will give you a longer time horizon to accumulate wealth through rental income and appreciation. Additionally, it is important to invest in areas that are likely to see strong population and economic growth in the future, such as major cities like Mumbai, Delhi, and Bangalore.

Another strategy is to invest in multiple properties. This will allow you to spread risk and increase your chances of success. Additionally, owning multiple properties can provide a steady stream of rental income, which can be used to pay off mortgages and build wealth over time.

Another way to invest in real estate is by investing in a Real Estate Investment Trust (REIT). REITs are publicly traded companies that own and operate income-producing real estate. They are required to pay out at least 90% of their taxable income to shareholders in the form of dividends, which can provide a steady stream of passive income.

It's also important to seek professional advice and guidance when investing in real estate. This can help you make informed decisions and avoid costly mistakes.

In summary, becoming a real estate millionaire in India requires a long-term investment strategy, an understanding of the Indian real estate market, and a willingness to take calculated risks. Investing in areas that are likely to see strong population and economic growth, owning multiple properties, investing in REITs, and seeking professional advice are key to success.

And Yess, Just Put in your Hardwork and give it some years to compound, and you will be a real estate millionaire sooooon!

"All the best for your journey to become a Real Estate Millionaire, you can, and you will definitely do it!!"

CHAPTER FIVE

Real Estate Investment Trust (REIT)

"Are you tired of boring old stocks and bonds? Want to invest in something more exciting, like real estate? Well, have you heard of Real Estate Investment Trusts (REIT)? Think of them as the wild child of the investment world - they let you play in the real estate market without having to deal with the hassles of being a landlord!" And one more fun fact-You can start your investment in REITs with just Rs. 400-500/-

Now, excited!! So, let's start our REIT journey:

Firstly, let's see what are REITs?

REITs: A Real Estate Investment Trust is a type of investment vehicle that allows individuals like you and me to invest in a portfolio of real estate assets, such as commercial properties, residential buildings, and mortgages. REITs are designed to provide investors with a way to access the benefits of real estate investing without the need for significant capital or the burden of managing the properties themselves. It is like a mutual fund where a pool of investors bring in money together and then the fund manager invests that money and distribute the returns/profits to investors. Similar is the case with REITs, where this REIT collects money from individual investors and then invest that big pool of money in real estate properties, and manage everything, the rentals etc. and after taking their fees, they give rental yield (in form of dividends) and also capital appreciation to their investors.

Here are some key features and characteristics of REITs:

1. Structure:

REITs are typically structured as corporations or trusts and are traded on stock exchanges like other securities. REITs in India are regulated by (SEBI)

Securities and Exchange Board of India and by **Securities and Exchange Commission** (SEC) in the United States. As a trust, REITs are owned by its shareholders and managed by trustees, while as a corporation, REITs are owned by its shareholders and managed by a board of directors and management team. REITs own a portfolio of real estate assets, which may include commercial properties, residential buildings, and mortgages. These assets generate income through rental income, mortgage interest, and other sources. REITs are typically managed by a professional management team, which is responsible for the day-to-day operations and management of the REIT's assets. This team is often responsible for acquiring, developing, and managing the REIT's properties.

2. Diversification:

REITs provide diversification across different properties, sectors, and regions, which can help to reduce risk. According to SEBI regulations, REITs in India need to follow this guideline: They have to invest at least 80% of total amount in complete properties and income generating properties, and remaining 20% they can invest in under-construction properties or equity shares or mortgage backed securities etc. This rule is to protect retail investors from risky investments. From this, I think you must have got some idea about how much risky or how much returns can you expect from REITs, but no worries, I will also discuss in detail about returns and risk you can expect further in this chapter.

3. Income:

REITs generate income through rental income, mortgage interest, and other sources. This income is then distributed to shareholders in the form of dividends. REITs are required to distribute at least 90% of their taxable income or cash flow generated through rents to unit holders (shareholders) [In REITs, investors can buy number of units, concept is similar, in case of equity, we call them number of shares] in the form of dividends. This income distribution is designed to provide shareholders with a steady stream of income from their investment in the REIT.

4. Tax benefits:

REITs offer certain tax benefits, such as deducting dividends paid to shareholders as a business expense. REITs are generally taxed as pass-through entities, which means that the REIT itself is not taxed on its income. Instead, the income is passed through to shareholders and taxed at the individual level. REITs also have some benefits in terms of tax deductions and depreciation, but it may vary depending on the country or jurisdiction. In India, REITs are offered some tax exemptions on their rental income, leasing etc. which reduces their tax liability and generate higher income for unit holders/ investors.

Now, for investors, there are four ways here to make money:

(i) Dividends (ii) Return of Capital by SPV (Amortization of Special purpose vehicle debt) (iii) Capital Gains (iv) Interest

So, now for investor, all these incomes are taxable, per investor's income tax slab, except this Return of Capital by SPV, it is tax-free. In case of Capital gains, similarly like stocks, short term capital gains are taxed at 15% (For less than 1 year), long term capital gains are taxed at 10% (Hold for more than 1 year) and now tax paid on dividends is different from REIT to REIT.

According to government guidelines in India, if the REIT in which you are investing, if it's SPV has opted for a lower tax regime or tax exemption, then tax becomes deductible at investor's hands, otherwise, if your REIT, in which you are investing your money, if it's SPV has not opted for a lower-tax regime, then your dividends are tax-exempt in that case in your (Investors') hands.

So, this taxation was a little bit complicated in this case, but I think you should have understood the broader story after reading this. Also, if there is no exemption present, then, In India, Real Estate Investment Trusts (REITs) are subject to tax on the income earned by the trust. The income is taxed at the rate of 30% for domestic REITs and 40% for foreign REITs. Dividends paid to unit holders are also subject to a dividend distribution tax (DDT) of 20%.

Additionally, capital gains tax may also be applicable on the sale of units in a REIT, but for now there are tax-exemptions present because our govt. want this to grow, and today you can get these tax benefits, which we have seen above.

(You can consult with your tax professional to understand the specific tax implications of investing in a REIT in India.)

5. Regulation:

REITs are subject to regulatory oversight, including rules regarding the distribution of dividends and the management of assets. These regulations are designed to protect investors and ensure that REITs are managed in a transparent and accountable manner. They are traded on stock exchanges, and are subject to regulation. They are regulated by SEBI in the India, and SEC in the USA. The regulations for REITs in India were first issued by SEBI in 2014 and were later amended in 2019.

According to the regulations, REITs in India must have a minimum of 10 investors and a minimum net worth of INR 500 crore (approximately $68 million). Additionally, the REIT must have at least 3 properties and the value of these properties must be at least INR 250 crore (approximately $34 million). The REITs in India also have to comply with certain listing requirements, such as listing on a stock exchange and maintaining a minimum public shareholding of 25%.

Moreover, the REITs are also required to distribute at least 90% of their distributable cash flow as dividends to the unit holders. And to invest their 80% in complete and income generating projects.

Furthermore, the REITs in India are also subject to strict regulations on related party transactions, to ensure that the REITs are not exploited for the benefit of a few individuals or entities. It is worth noting that REITs are still in the nascent stage in India and the regulations are being continually updated to encourage the growth of the REIT market.

6. Types:

There are different types of REITs, including equity REITs which own and operate properties, mortgage REITs which invest in mortgages and other real estate-related debt, hybrid REITs, which have a combination of both and infrastructure REITs which hold ownership in infrastructure assets; such as cell towers, data centers, and toll roads.

7. Risk:

As with any investment, REITs carry risk. The value of REITs can be affected by changes in the real estate market, interest rates, and the overall economy. Investors must research and consider their risk tolerance before investing in a REIT.

Benefits of REITs:

Real estate investment trusts (REITs) provide several benefits for common investors. One of the main benefits is the ability to invest in real estate without the need to buy and manage property directly. REITs allow investors to own shares in a trust that owns and manages income-producing real estate, such as office buildings, apartments, and shopping centers. This allows individual investors to gain exposure to the real estate market and earn income from rental properties without the hassle of being a landlord. REITs also offer diversification benefits, as they provide a way to invest in real estate as part of a balanced portfolio.

Additionally, REITs are required to pay out at least 90% of their taxable income to shareholders as dividends, which can provide a steady stream of income for investors. And individual investors also do not need to own very big capital, they can start investing in REITs with just Rs. 400-500/- per unit. This thing was not possible few years back, and everyone thought that for investing in real estate, you must need a massive amount, which was true back then, but now, you can surely enjoy this privilege of becoming a real estate investor at a very less amount. Of course, you will receive benefits according to the amount you have invested in, but yes, it still gives you a chance to invest in some safer assets like real estate. And apart from these, there are many other benefits of REITs like liquidity (REITs are publicly traded and can be bought and sold on stock exchanges, which makes them more liquid than investing directly in property) and Professional management (REITs are managed by professional teams, which can help to reduce the risks associated with investing in real estate) etc.

However, REITs may not be suitable for all kinds of investors. They tend to be more suitable for those who are looking for a steady income stream, and are comfortable with the risks associated with investing in the real estate market. REITs are not suitable for investors who are looking for high growth potential, as they tend to be more focused on income generation.

Also, REITs are typically considered to be more conservative investments, and may not be suitable for investors who are looking for higher returns and are willing to take on more risk. It is important for investors to consider their own investment goals, risk tolerance and financial situation before investing in REITs.

Now, we have seen what are REITs, their structure, some other features related to REITs, their benefits, so now you will be saying "Gurcharan, enough! Now just tell us how to invest in REITs and what to look for, how to identify good REITs, which parameters to look? How to do their analysis" Okay, okay, so let's now dive into that:

But before that, I want to explain you these three to four terms, which will help you in analyzing REITs:

1. Net Asset Value (NAV) in a Real Estate Investment Trust (REIT) is a measure of the value of the assets of the trust minus its liabilities. NAV per unit is calculated by dividing the total value of the trust's assets by the number of shares outstanding. This value is used to determine the price at which shares of the REIT can be bought or sold on the stock market. It is similar to the concept of book value for a traditional company.

Net Asset Value = Gross Asset Value - Liabilities/Debt

Net asset value

Particulars (₹ million)	March 31, 2021
Gross Asset Value (GAV)[2,3]	466,051
Add: Other Assets	81,820
Less: Other Liabilities	(74,298)
Less: Gross Debt	(106,223)
Net Asset Value (NAV)	367,350
Number of Units	947,893,743
NAV per Unit (₹)	387.54

This is a picture from financial statements of India's best REIT (Embassy REIT) for Annual FY21, so you can see from here clearly, that how we calculate NAV.

Some of you might have invested in mutual funds, so you must be knowing that NAV of a mutual fund is declared daily, but that does not make sense in case of a REIT, as it makes no practicals sense to calculate a property's value on a daily basis. So, in this case, NAV is calculated every six months.

So, for the people who are reading this term (NAV) for the first time, you can think about it like a share price. (NAV price ~ Share price) for understanding. So, NAV is a measure of the value of an investment company's assets minus its liabilities. It is used to determine the value of a unit or share in a mutual fund or exchange-traded fund (ETF) and now in case of REITs.

For example, if a mutual fund has $10 million in assets and $2 million in liabilities, its NAV per share would be ($10 million - $2 million) / the number of shares outstanding. If the fund has 1 million shares outstanding, the NAV per share would be $8. So, for each share you own, you would be entitled to a share in $8 of the fund's assets.

We will discuss on it further in analyzing REITs section.

2. Weighted average lease expiry (WALE) is a metric used to measure the average remaining length of leases for a real estate investment trust (REIT). It is calculated by taking the total lease expiry for all properties within a REIT's portfolio and dividing it by the total rental income generated by those properties. The result is the average number of years remaining on all leases within the portfolio.

3. Occupancy rate in the case of REITs (Real Estate Investment Trusts) refers to the percentage of leased or occupied space within a REIT's portfolio of properties. It is a measure of the effectiveness of a REIT in leasing its properties to tenants.

4. A REIT's **distribution yield** is a measure of its dividend income relative to its current stock price. It is calculated by dividing the annual dividends per share by the current stock price and expressed as a percentage. The distribution yield can be used as a way to compare the income-generating potential of different REITs.

5. Portfolio Quality consists of location and tenants dependencies i.e. geographical spread and diversity (In how many cities, this REIT has properties etc. and percentage). Similarly, number of tenants and dependencies on those (in %).

Now after getting an insight into these terms, let's now deep dive into how to analyze and select REITs.

Analyzing REITs :

Although there are not much options to select from in India yet, only three main REITs (Embassy Office Parks REIT (a joint venture between Blackstone and Embassy group), Mindspace Business Parks REIT, Brookfield India Real Estate Trust REIT) are present currently in India, but in the future, this number will definitely grow as The Indian government announced plans to open up the REIT market in India in 2019, and several companies have expressed interest in launching REITs. So, now, There are several things to consider when purchasing a unit in a Real Estate Investment Trust (REIT). Some of the most important things to check include:

1. Diversification:

It is important to ensure that the REIT you are considering investing in has a diversified portfolio of properties across different sectors, such as retail, office, and residential.

2. Occupancy rate:

Look for REITs that have high occupancy rates, as this indicates a strong demand for the properties they own. A high occupancy rate indicates that the REIT is successful in leasing its properties and generating income, while a low occupancy rate may indicate difficulty in leasing properties and lower income potential for investors. Typically, REITs aim for occupancy rates of at least 90%.

3. Financial performance:

Review the REIT's financial statements to ensure they have a consistent history of paying dividends and have a strong financial position.

4. Management team:

Research the management team and their track record of successfully managing and growing the REIT.

5. Fees:

Compare the fees associated with the REIT to others in the market to ensure they are reasonable and fair.

6. Risk profile:

Understand the risk profile of the REIT and ensure it aligns with your investment goals and risk tolerance.

7. Valuation:

Compare the price of the REIT to its net asset value (NAV) and ensure that it is reasonably priced. Now, NAV in isolation may tell you nothing, but when you compare it with market value of that REIT, you will definitely get an idea whether to purchase this REIT or not. So, Generally from my observation, Market value to NAV ratio gives the conclusion that Indian REITs typically trade at a 12-15% discount, now you will see in market, sometimes, it will be available at some premium, and at some times, it will be available at deep discounts, so there you can exit or enter these REITs respectively and also a bonus point here is, we know NAV of a REIT is updated every 6 months, but as your experience with REITs will grow, you will also be able to identify some arbitrage opportunities in this. So, you can see this from NAV, that is it overpriced or underpriced, i.e. is it right time to sell or buy this REIT?

8. Distribution yield:

A REIT's distribution yield is a measure of its dividend income relative to its current stock price. It is calculated by dividing the annual dividends per share by the current stock price and expressed as a percentage. The distribution yield can be used as a way to compare the income-generating potential of different REITs. However, it's important to keep in mind that a high distribution yield may also indicate that the REIT's stock price has decreased and may be at risk of further decline. This can be used for the comparison of potential of different REITs to generate income.

9. *WALE:*

It is an important metric for REIT investors because it indicates the stability and predictability of a REIT's cash flow. A REIT with a long WALE is considered less risky than one with a short WALE, because it is more likely to generate consistent rental income over a longer period of time. Additionally, if a REIT has a long WALE, it will have more time to find new tenants or renegotiate leases when they expire, which can help to mitigate the risk of vacancy. For example, if a REIT has a portfolio of properties with a total lease expiry of 10 years, and the total rental income generated by those properties is $100,000 per year, the WALE would be 10 years. It is important to keep in mind that, WALE is not a perfect measure, it can be affected by how leases are structured and the terms of the lease. Additionally, the WALE of a REIT can vary depending on the type of properties it holds. For example, a REIT that holds primarily retail properties may have a shorter WALE than a REIT that holds primarily office properties, because retail leases tend to be shorter.

10. It is also a good idea to consult with your financial advisor before making any investment decisions.

Present and Future of REITs in India:

Currently, as of 2022, there are three REITs present in India. Embassy Office Parks REIT, Mindspace Business Parks REIT, Brookfield India Real Estate Trust REIT.

These all are a public-traded trust in India that owns and operates a portfolio of mostly office properties in the country. They every quarter and mainly every year, release their financial statements to public. For beginners, these are like publicly listed companies, which invest in real estates and gives you your share in rent as dividends.

Embassy Office Parks REIT is the first REIT to be listed in India and its listing in April 2019 on the National Stock Exchange of India and BSE Limited. This REIT's portfolio includes over 34 million square feet of office space across several properties in key markets in India, such as Bengaluru, Pune, and the National Capital Region.

Similarly, **Mindspace Business Parks REIT's** portfolio includes around 17 million square feet of office space across several properties in key markets in India, such as Mumbai, Hyderabad, and Pune.

Also, **Brookfield's REIT** also includes a big portfolio of 17-18 Million square feet and major cities are Mumbai, Pune, Pawai etc. The properties are leased to a diverse group of tenants in various industries, including technology, engineering, and financial services. This is the present state of REITs in our country.

Now, The future of Real Estate Investment Trusts (REITs) in India is expected to be much more positive, as the Indian government has been working to establish a favorable regulatory environment for REITs.

REITs will have a bright future in India, according to me, because:

1. Government support: The Indian government has taken several steps to encourage the growth of the REIT market, such as providing tax incentives and simplifying regulations.

2. Growing market: The Indian real estate market is growing, and the emergence of REITs will provide a new source of funding for developers, which will help to spur further growth in the sector.

3. Increased investment opportunities: REITs will provide investors with new opportunities to invest in the Indian real estate market, which was previously difficult for retail investors.

4. Low-cost investment: REITs will allow investors to invest in real estate at a relatively low cost, as compared to buying property directly.

5. Risk management: REITs will help to manage risks in the real estate market, as the trust structure allows for the diversification of investments across multiple properties.

However, there are also some challenges that the REIT market in India will face, such as lack of transparency, lack of liquidity and low investor awareness.

It is important that the government and industry players continue to work to address these challenges to ensure the continued growth and success of the REIT market in India.

CHAPTER SIX

Let's Explore Prop-Tech

Watching Shark Tank? Or Have an interest in startups? Are you a techie? In any of the three cases, you will love this section. See, as you all know, Tech is enabling every business today, and it's changing the way traditional businesses do their business. Now, Attention of viewers, traction, number of users etc. are more relevant terms for VCs rather than Profit, EBITDA etc. No problem, we can talk about startups and this industry any other day, let me know directly jump to the talk of the town, After Ed-Tech and Fin-Tech, let's welcome **Prop-Tech**, I think now all of you will be getting an idea about this proptech. Let us now deep dive into it.

Proptech (property technology),

refers to the use of technology to improve and innovate processes and services in the real estate industry. This can include everything from online platforms for buying and selling property, to the use of data analytics and building management systems to improve the efficiency and sustainability of buildings. Some examples of proptech include online real estate marketplaces, virtual and augmented reality tools for property viewings, and smart home technology for building management. Let's see in some detail:

So, basically Proptech, short for property technology, is a term used to describe the intersection of technology and real estate. It refers to the use of technology to improve and innovate processes and services in the real estate industry. Proptech companies use technology to address various aspects of the real estate industry, including property search and discovery, transaction management, property management, and building management.

One of the key trends in proptech is the use of big data and analytics to improve decision-making and identify new opportunities in the market. By collecting and analyzing large amounts of data on property prices, trends, and demand, proptech companies can help real estate professionals make better decisions and identify new opportunities. Proptech solutions can help to improve the efficiency of the real estate industry, increase transparency, and reduce costs. This can benefit both real estate professionals and consumers.

For example, proptech solutions can make it easier for consumers to find and purchase properties, and can help real estate professionals to market and manage properties more effectively.

Another trend in proptech is the use of blockchain technology to improve transparency and security in property transactions. Blockchain technology can be used to create a tamper-proof digital ledger of property ownership and transaction history, which can improve the transparency and security of property transactions.

Overall, proptech is an exciting and rapidly growing field that has the potential to revolutionize the way we think about and interact with real estate. It is a combination of technology, real estate and innovation that is changing the way the industry operates and making it more efficient, transparent and customer-friendly.

Now, after knowing what is Proptech, let's see **how Proptech is enabling the real estate industry:** Proptech, or property technology, is enabling the real estate industry in a number of ways.

Some of the ways include:

1. Improved Efficiency:

Proptech tools and platforms can automate many of the manual processes involved in buying and selling property, such as property search, document management, and contract execution, making it easier and faster for buyers and sellers to complete transactions.

2. Increased Transparency:

Proptech can provide more detailed and accurate information about properties, making it easier for buyers to compare properties and make informed decisions.

3. Better Marketing:

Proptech can help real estate companies and agents to market their properties more effectively, using virtual and augmented reality tools, social media, and data analytics to reach a wider audience and create more engaging content.

4. Better Building Management:

Prop-Tech solutions can help the building managers to monitor and optimize energy consumption, reduce costs, and improve the comfort and safety of building occupants.

5. Better customer experience:

Prop-Tech solutions like virtual tours, 3D walkthroughs, AR/VR viewings, and online document signing, are making it much easier for customers to interact with properties, giving them a much better experience compared to traditional methods.

6. Better data analytics:

Proptech is also providing more data and insights to the real estate industry, which can help companies make better decisions and identify new opportunities in the market.

Overall, proptech is helping to make the real estate industry more efficient, transparent, and customer-friendly, while also providing new opportunities for growth and innovation.

Let's now see some examples of PropTech startups and businesses:

So, There are several Indian startups in the proptech space. Some examples include:

1. Housing.com:

An online real estate marketplace that allows users to search for properties, compare prices, and connect with agents.

2. NoBroker:

An online platform that connects property owners and renters directly, eliminating the need for a traditional broker.

3. Square Yards:

An online real estate platform that provides end-to-end services for buying and selling property, including property search, legal assistance, and home loans.

4. Smartowner:

A platform that allows investors to buy shares in commercial and residential properties and earn rental income.

5. CasaOne:

Furniture rental start-up, that allows customers to rent furniture and home decor for short-term or long-term periods.

These are just a few examples of the proptech companies in India, the industry is growing and there are many more startups emerging in this space.

Let's see the **business models** of some of these companies in detail:

So, first we have a unicorn startup in our list, **NoBroker**.

NoBroker is an online platform that connects property owners and renters directly, eliminating the need for a traditional broker. The company operates on a commission-free business model, which means that it does not charge any fees or commissions to either the property owner or the tenant for facilitating a rental transaction. Instead, it generates revenue through a variety of other channels.

One of the main sources of revenue for NoBroker is its "Home Services" offering, which provides a range of services such as home cleaning, painting, and plumbing to both property owners and renters. The company charges a fee for these services, which can be paid directly through the NoBroker platform.

Another source of revenue is its "NoBrokerHood" feature, which is a social networking platform for neighbors that aims to build a community of verified and trusted tenants and owners. NoBroker charges a fee to property owners and tenants who want to use this feature.

NoBroker also offers home rental insurance, personal accident insurance and other such services which generates revenue for the company. NoBroker's business model is different from traditional real estate agents, which rely on commissions from property transactions. Instead, the company aims to generate revenue through a variety of other channels, including home services and social networking, while providing a commission-free service to users.

Next, we have in the list is, you must have heard its name, it is **MagicBricks.**

Magicbricks is an online real estate platform that allows users to search for properties, compare prices, and connect with agents. The company operates on a revenue-sharing business model, which means that it earns money by charging a fee to property owners and agents for listing their properties on the platform and for other services.

One of the main sources of revenue for Magicbricks is its property listing service. Property owners and agents can list their properties on the platform for a fee, and these listings will be visible to users who are searching for properties. The fee for listing a property can vary depending on the type of property, the location, and the duration of the listing.

Another source of revenue for Magicbricks is its advertising services. The platform provides advertising opportunities to builders, developers, and other businesses that are related to the real estate industry. These businesses can advertise their projects, products, and services on the platform and pay Magicbricks a fee for this service. The company also offers premium services such as "Featured Property" where the property is highlighted and gets more visibility, "Priority Listing" where the property is on top of the search result, "Exclusive Listing" where the property is only listed on Magicbricks and many more. These premium services come with a fee.

Magicbricks generates revenue by providing a platform for property owners and agents to list their properties and connect with potential buyers, and by providing advertising opportunities for businesses related to the real estate industry. The company earns money by charging a fee for these services.

Next, we have is, **PropTiger.**

PropTiger is an online real estate platform that provides end-to-end services for buying and selling property, including property search, legal assistance, and home loans. The company operates on a revenue-sharing business model, which means that it earns money by charging a fee to property developers, builders and agents for listing their properties on the platform and for other services.

One of the main sources of revenue for PropTiger is its property listing service. Property developers, builders and agents can list their properties on the platform for a fee, and these listings will be visible to users who are searching for properties. The fee for listing a property can vary depending on the type of property, the location, and the duration of the listing.

Another source of revenue for PropTiger is its advertising services. The platform provides advertising opportunities to builders, developers, and other businesses that are related to the real estate industry. These businesses can advertise their projects, products, and services on the platform and pay PropTiger a fee for this service. PropTiger also generates revenue from its home loan service. The company partners with various banks and financial institutions to provide home loans to its customers. The company earns a commission from these financial institutions for every home loan that is disbursed through its platform. PropTiger also offers value-added services such as property valuations, legal assistance, and home-buying advice to its customers. These services are provided on a paid basis.

PropTiger's business model is based on generating revenue by providing a platform for property developers, builders and agents to list their properties and connect with potential buyers, and by providing advertising opportunities and value-added services for businesses related to the real estate industry. The company earns money by charging a fee for these services.

Next is, **Housing.com**. It is an online real estate marketplace that allows users to search for properties, compare prices, and connect with agents. The company operates on a revenue-sharing business model, which means that it earns money by charging a fee to property developers, builders and agents for listing their properties on the platform and for other services.

One of the main sources of revenue for Housing.com is its property listing service. Property developers, builders and agents can list their properties on the platform for a fee, and these listings will be visible to users who are searching for properties. The fee for listing a property can vary depending on the type of property, the location, and the duration of the listing.

Another source of revenue for Housing.com is its advertising services. The platform provides advertising opportunities to builders, developers, and other businesses that are related to the real estate industry. These businesses can advertise their projects, products, and services on the platform and pay Housing.com a fee for this service. Housing.com also generates revenue from its home loan service. The company partners with various banks and financial institutions to provide home loans to its customers. The company earns a commission from these financial institutions for every home loan that is disbursed through its platform. Housing.com also offers value-added services such as property valuations, legal assistance, and home-buying advice to its customers. These services are provided on a paid basis.

Housing.com's business model is based on generating revenue by providing a platform for property developers, builders and agents to list their properties and connect with potential buyers, and by providing advertising opportunities and value-added services for businesses related to the real estate industry. The company earns money by charging a fee for these services.

Next we have is, this is one of my favorites, **CasaOne**.

CasaOne is a furniture rental start-up that allows customers to rent furniture and home decor for short-term or long-term periods. The company operates on a subscription based business model, which means that customers pay a monthly fee to rent furniture, and the company provides delivery, installation, and maintenance services.

The main source of revenue for CasaOne is the rental fees paid by customers. Customers can choose from a variety of rental plans, which can include different furniture styles, sizes, and rental periods. The rental fees are based on the value of the furniture, the rental period, and the services provided by the company. CasaOne also generates revenue from additional services such as installation, maintenance, and moving services. Customers can choose to purchase these services separately or as part of a package. For example, customers can choose to have furniture installed in their home or office, or they can opt for the company to move furniture from one location to another.

Another source of revenue for CasaOne is its "Furniture as a Service" (FaaS) offering, which allows customers to rent furniture as part of a flexible subscription service. This is targeted at businesses, like startups and co-working spaces, that need furniture but don't want to make a long-term commitment.

CasaOne's business model is different from traditional furniture retailers, which rely on selling furniture outright. Instead, the company aims to generate revenue by providing a flexible, subscription-based service that allows customers to rent furniture on a short-term or long-term basis. This allows customers to try out different furniture styles, avoid the commitment of buying furniture outright, and only pay for what they use.

So, there are many other more players in this industry, doing well, but others all have a typically same business model with some variations. Someone is working on A1, someone is on A2, someone is on A3,4 and so on, but all they are trying to do is help customers solve their problems in this real estate sector with the help of or by using technology.

So, a typical proptech company uses technology to improve and streamline various aspects of the real estate industry, such as property management, buying and selling, and tenant interactions. Their business model can involve creating and selling software or platforms to help landlords, property managers, and other real estate professionals manage their properties more efficiently, as well as providing services such as online rental listings, tenant screening, and rent collection.

They may also generate revenue through commissions on property sales or by charging a subscription fee for access to their platform or services. And the rest I leave on you, as an exercise, to find some more startups doing good in this Prop-Tech industry and do observe their business models, what problem they are trying to solve, is there any positive change now in industry because of them, are they able to create an impact, will they be able to survive? Everything, just analyze these things. You will definitely learn a lot.

And, now at the end of this chapter, for those of you who have gained some interest in proptech after reading this, and want to make their own startups in proptech industry, let me give you some tips:

Starting your own proptech startup can be a challenging but rewarding endeavor. So, these are some steps you can take to get started:

1. Identify a problem or opportunity: To start a successful proptech startup, you need to identify a problem or opportunity in the real estate industry that you can solve or capitalize on. This might involve conducting market research, talking to industry experts, and identifying gaps in the market that existing solutions are not addressing.

2. Develop a unique solution: Once you have identified a problem or opportunity, you need to develop a unique solution that addresses it. This might involve creating a new platform, developing a new technology, or finding a new way to use existing technologies.

3. Build a team: Starting a proptech startup requires a diverse set of skills and expertise, so it's important to build a team of people with the right skills and experience to help you bring your solution to market.

4. Raise Funds: Starting a startup requires money, as you need to pay your team and cover other expenses. You can raise funds through various ways such as bootstrapping, seeking angel investors or venture capitalists or crowdfunding.

5. Develop a prototype: Once you have a solid idea and a team in place, you should develop a prototype of your solution to test and validate your concept. This will help you identify any problems with your solution and make any necessary changes before you launch.

6. Launch and grow: Once your solution is ready, you can launch it and start growing your business. This may involve developing marketing and sales strategies, building partnerships and collaborations, and continuously seeking feedback from customers to improve your product.

Starting a proptech startup can be a challenging process, but with a clear vision, a solid business plan, and a dedicated team, you can create a successful proptech company. All the very best to you!

CHAPTER SEVEN

Business Models of Some Companies Working in Real Estate

The four biggest real estate companies in the world are **Brookfield Asset Management** (This Canadian company is one of the largest alternative asset managers in the world, with a focus on real estate, infrastructure, and renewable energy. It has a diverse portfolio of properties and investments in various countries, including the United States, Canada, and Europe), **Prologis** (This American company is one of the largest owners and operators of industrial real estate in the world, with a portfolio of properties in more than 19 countries), **Blackstone** (This American company is one of the largest alternative investment managers in the world, with a focus on real estate, private equity, hedge funds, and credit. It has a diverse portfolio of properties and investments in various countries, including the United States, Europe, and Asia), **CBRE Group** (This American company is one of the largest commercial real estate services and investment firms in the world, providing services such as property management, leasing, valuation, and investment management. It operates in more than 90 countries worldwide).

It's worth noting that these companies are large and diversified, they are not limited to real estate only, they operate in multiple sectors and have many other businesses as well. Additionally, the ranking of these companies may change over time as the industry is constantly evolving.

Here's a brief overview of the business models of these four biggest real estate companies in the world:

1. Brookfield Asset Management:

Brookfield's business model is focused on acquiring and managing a diverse portfolio of assets across multiple sectors, including real estate, infrastructure, and renewable energy. They typically invest in assets that generate stable cash flows, such as office buildings, shopping centers, and power generation facilities. They also invest in development projects, such as building new properties or upgrading existing ones. They generate revenue through rental income and capital appreciation.

2. Prologis:

Prologis is primarily focused on the industrial real estate sector, specifically on the development, acquisition, and management of logistics facilities, warehouses and distribution centers. They generate revenue through rental income and capital appreciation. They also have a growing business in providing logistics services, such as last-mile delivery and e-commerce fulfillment.

3. Blackstone:

Blackstone's business model is focused on investing in a wide range of assets, including real estate, private equity, hedge funds, and credit. The company's real estate business includes investing in properties, developing new properties, and managing properties for its own portfolio or for other investors. They generate revenue through rental income, capital appreciation, and management fees.

4. CBRE Group:

CBRE operates primarily as a commercial real estate services and investment firm, providing services such as property management, leasing, valuation, and investment management. It generates revenue through the fees it charges for these services, as well as through its own investments in properties and funds. Additionally, CBRE has a growing business in providing consulting services, such as strategic planning, project management, and sustainability consulting.

It's worth noting that these companies have a complex business model and their revenue streams are not limited to what I mentioned above. They also have other businesses that are not directly related to real estate. Additionally, the business models of these companies may change over time as the industry evolves.

Now, let's talk about some Indian companies or the companies which are doing pretty well in Indian Real Estate Sector.

If you love cricket, you would have definitely heard of the next name I am going to talk about, Remember the first or second season of IPL, maybe 2008 or 2009, who were the sponsors, any guesses? Yes DLF, right! And if you are from Delhi-NCR or nearby area, you must have visited at least once this big DLF mall. So, this company is DLF.

DLF Limited,

is one of the largest real estate development companies in India, with a focus on residential, commercial, and retail properties.

DLF's business model is primarily based on the development and sale of residential and commercial properties. They typically acquire land, obtain necessary approvals and then develop the land into residential and commercial projects such as townships, malls, office buildings, and apartments. They also generate revenue through rental income from commercial properties such as shopping malls and office buildings. DLF also has a presence in the hospitality sector and has developed several luxury hotels and resorts.

In addition to the development and sale of properties, DLF also generates revenue through its property management services, which includes managing and leasing of commercial and residential properties. DLF has also diversified into other businesses such as infrastructure development and power generation, but the real estate development and services continue to be the core business of the company.

It's worth noting that DLF's business model may change over time as the industry and the company evolves.

Next in the list we have, I think you have never expected that company in the list of Real Estate business, and I am sure you would have heard that company's name for almirahs, very safe lockers etc. So, this company is Godrej.

Godrej Properties,

is one of the leading real estate development companies in India, with a focus on residential and commercial properties.

The business model of Godrej Properties is primarily based on the development and sale of residential and commercial properties. They typically acquire land, obtain necessary approvals and then develop the land into residential and commercial projects such as townships, malls, office buildings, and apartments. They also generate revenue through rental income from commercial properties such as shopping malls and office buildings. Godrej Properties also has a presence in the hospitality sector and has developed several luxury hotels and resorts.

In addition to the development and sale of properties, Godrej Properties also generates revenue through its property management services, which includes managing and leasing of commercial and residential properties. Godrej Properties has a diversified portfolio of projects across multiple segments and geographies, which allows them to mitigate risk and capitalize on growth opportunities. They also have a strong focus on sustainability and eco-friendly construction practices.

It's worth noting that Godrej Properties's business model may change over time as the industry and the company evolves.

Next, we have is, **Oberoi Realty**.

Oberoi Realty,

is one of the leading real estate development companies in India, with a focus on luxury residential, commercial, and hospitality properties.

The business model of Oberoi Realty is primarily based on the development and sale of luxury residential and commercial properties. They typically acquire land, obtain necessary approvals, and then develop the land into luxury residential and commercial projects such as townships, malls, office buildings, and apartments. They also generate revenue through rental income from commercial properties such as shopping malls and office buildings. Oberoi Realty also has a presence in the hospitality sector and has developed several luxury hotels and resorts.

In addition to the development and sale of properties, Oberoi Realty also generates revenue through its property management services, which includes managing and leasing of commercial and residential properties.

Oberoi Realty is known for their luxury projects, which are designed to cater to high-end customers. They have a strong reputation for quality and luxury, which helps them attract premium pricing for their projects. They also have a strong focus on sustainability and eco-friendly construction practices.

It's worth noting that Oberoi Realty's business model may change over time as the industry and the company evolves.

Now, I know all of you must have eaten McDonald's burger or fries combo with coke, but what if I tell you that **McDonald's** is not a burger company, nor it is any fries, basically it's not a food company. It **is a Real-Estate company**. Shocked!? Let's see how,

Balance Sheet
All numbers in thousands

Breakdown	12/30/2021	12/30/2020	12/30/2019
⌄ Total Assets	53,854,300	52,626,800	47,510,800
> Current Assets	7,148,500	6,243,200	3,557,900
⌄ Total non-current assets	46,705,800	46,383,600	43,952,900
> Net PPE	38,272,600	38,785,900	37,421,200
> Goodwill And Other Intang…	2,782,500	2,773,100	2,677,400
> Investments And Advances	1,201,200	1,297,200	1,270,300
Other Non Current Assets	4,449,500	3,527,400	2,584,000
> Total Liabilities Net Minority Int…	58,455,300	60,451,700	55,721,100
> Total Equity Gross Minority Inte…	-4,601,000	-7,824,900	-8,210,300

Figure from Yahoo Finance of McDonald's Balance Sheet

You saw these PPE, that's Property, Plant and Equipments, So from here you can see that McDonalds has this much property (Around $40 billion). Can you calculate the rental income on this much property? So the business model of McDonalds is like this. McDonalds own the property, they buy the property before giving it to franchisee. Then, they give these properties to franchisees on lease, hence generating a massive rental income. These franchisees then operate McDonald's restaurants on the properties that they get on lease and McDonalds own. So, McDonald's makes money from both the sale of food and from collecting rent and royalties from its franchisees.

In other words, McDonald's generates a significant portion of its revenue from the sale and lease of real estate to its franchisees, making it a real estate company in addition to a fast food chain.

Ever saw this ad, "Habibi, Come to Dubai!!", Yes, As you all know Dubai is famous for its big skyscrapers, big buildings and some wonderful buildings, so we are talking about real estate and the real wonders of real estate you will see in Dubai. I personally love Dubai's buildings, they have super-infrastructure. So, let's talk about Dubai's biggest real estate company i.e. Emaar.

So, **Emaar Properties** is a Dubai-based real estate development company that makes money through a variety of different revenue streams. Some of the main ways that Emaar generates revenue include:

1. **Property sales:** Emaar develops and sells residential, commercial, and retail properties, such as apartments, villas, and office buildings. This is a primary source of revenue for the company.

2. **Rental income:** Emaar also generates revenue from rental income on properties that it owns, such as office buildings and shopping centers.

3. **Hospitality:** Emaar owns and operates a number of hotels and resorts, which generates revenue through room rentals, food and beverage, and other amenities.

4. **Property management:** Emaar manages and maintains a number of properties, including residential communities, and earns revenue through property management fees and other charges.

5. **Retail and leisure:** Emaar operates a number of retail and leisure destinations, such as malls and theme parks. It generates revenue through rent from tenants, ticket sales, and other activities.

6. **Others:** Emaar also generates revenue through land sales, joint ventures and other investments.

Overall, Emaar's business model is focused on developing and operating a diverse range of real estate assets, which generates revenue through a variety of sources, including property sales, rentals, and services.

Now, let's talk about business models of some construction based i.e. Real Estate Building and Developement companies:

First in the list is the world's biggest construction company i.e. Ferrovial.

Now, **Ferrovial** is a Spanish multinational infrastructure and services company. The company operates in several different sectors, including construction, airports, toll roads, and services.

Its business model is based on building, maintaining, and operating infrastructure and services for the public and private sectors.

In the construction sector, Ferrovial offers design and construction services for infrastructure and buildings projects. In the airports sector, it operates and manages airports worldwide. In the toll roads sector, it builds, maintains and operates highways and toll roads. In the services sector, Ferrovial provides services such as building and facility management, waste management, and street lighting maintenance. Ferrovial's main source of revenue comes from its concessions and services business, where it receives payments for maintaining and operating infrastructure assets, such as toll roads, airports, and other public facilities. Additionally, the company generates revenue through its construction and engineering business, by executing contracts and projects for the public and private sector.

In summary, Ferrovial's business model is based on providing a wide range of infrastructure and services through concessions, public-private partnerships, and traditional contracting methods, with a focus on long-term asset management and maintenance.

Let's talk about some Indian companies doing good in this space,

First is **L&T i.e. Larsen & Toubro**. It is an Indian multinational conglomerate company with interests in engineering, construction, manufacturing, and services.

In the construction sector, the company operates through several different business segments, including Buildings and Factories, Heavy Civil Infrastructure, Power Transmission and Distribution, and Water and Effluent Treatment.

The company's business model in construction is based on executing EPC (Engineering, Procurement, and Construction) contracts for various types of infrastructure and building projects. The company offers a wide range of services, including project management, design, engineering, procurement, and construction. L&T also provides operations and maintenance services for the assets they construct. L&T's main source of revenue in the construction business comes from executing EPC contracts for various types of projects such as, buildings, power plants, highways, bridges, ports, and airports. Additionally, the company generates revenue through its operations and maintenance business, by providing services for the assets they construct.

In summary, L&T's business model in construction is based on executing EPC contracts for infrastructure and building projects, and providing operations and maintenance services for the assets they construct. The company's extensive experience, technical expertise and strong reputation in the market for delivering projects on-time and within budget, which help the company to secure more contracts.

Next in the list is, **Reliance Infrastructure Limited (RInfra)** is an Indian engineering and construction company that operates in the infrastructure and real estate sectors. Similar to L&T, The company's business model in construction and real estate is based on executing EPC (Engineering, Procurement, and Construction) contracts for various types of infrastructure and building projects, and developing and selling residential and commercial real estate properties.

In the construction sector, RInfra offers a wide range of services, including project management, design, engineering, procurement, and construction for various types of projects such as power plants, highways, bridges, ports, airports, and metro rail projects. The company also provides operations and maintenance services for the assets they construct.

In the real estate sector, RInfra develops and sells residential and commercial properties through its subsidiary Reliance Realty. This includes the development of townships, malls, multiplexes and commercial buildings. RInfra's main source of revenue in the construction business comes from executing EPC contracts for various types of projects, and providing operations and maintenance services for the assets they construct. In the real estate business, the company generates revenue through the sale of residential and commercial properties, and through leasing and renting commercial properties.

In summary, RInfra's business model in construction and real estate is based on executing EPC contracts for infrastructure and building projects, providing operations and maintenance services for the assets they construct, and developing and selling residential and commercial real estate properties. The company's diversified business model helps it to mitigate the risk and maintain a steady flow of revenue.

Next we have is, our lovely, **The Tata Group**, a large Indian conglomerate, has a presence in the real estate business through several of its subsidiaries and joint ventures. The company's real estate portfolio includes residential and commercial properties, as well as hospitality and retail projects.

One of Tata Group's major real estate subsidiaries is Tata Housing Development Company Limited (THDC). THDC is engaged in the development of residential and commercial properties across India, and it offers a wide range of properties such as affordable housing, luxury housing, and gated communities. The company also has a presence in the international market, with projects in countries such as Maldives and Sri Lanka.

Another subsidiary of Tata Group involved in the real estate sector is Tata Realty and Infrastructure Limited (TRIL), which is involved in the development of infrastructure and real estate projects across India. The company focuses on developing integrated townships, commercial properties, and SEZs (Special Economic Zones). Tata Group also has a presence in the hospitality sector through Tata Hotels and Resorts, which operates a range of hotels and resorts across India.

In summary, Tata Group is involved in the real estate business through its subsidiary companies such as Tata Housing Development Company Limited, Tata Realty and Infrastructure Limited, which are involved in the development of residential, commercial and infrastructure projects across India and internationally, and in the hospitality sector through Tata Hotels and Resorts. The company's diverse business model allows it to have a steady flow of revenue and mitigate the risk.

Next, we have is, **Hindustan Construction Company (HCC)** is an Indian engineering and construction company that operates in several different sectors, including infrastructure, building and real estate, and power.

In the infrastructure sector, HCC executes EPC (Engineering, Procurement and Construction) contracts for various types of projects such as highways, bridges, ports, airports, and metro rail projects. The company also provides operations and maintenance services for the assets they construct.

In the building and real estate sector, HCC constructs and develops residential and commercial properties. They also provide services such as project management, design, engineering, procurement and construction for various types of building projects.

In the power sector, HCC is involved in the construction of power plants, including hydroelectric and thermal power projects.

HCC's main source of revenue comes from executing EPC contracts for various types of projects such as infrastructure, building and real estate, and power sector. Additionally, the company generates revenue through its operations and maintenance business, by providing services for the assets they construct. It also generates revenue by selling and renting the properties they develop in the building and real estate sector.

In summary, Hindustan Construction Company's business model is based on executing EPC contracts for various types of infrastructure and building projects, providing operations and maintenance services for the assets they construct, and developing and selling residential and commercial real estate properties in the building and real estate sector, and construction of power plants in the power sector. This diversified business model helps the company to have a steady flow of revenue and mitigate the risk.

So, Why I told you about these companies and that also when there are many similar things, similar functions of these companies, why I told you those things again and again, so the answer is to inspire you to read about some case studies on these companies and more companies in this industry. From previous 10 pages, by reading about these companies, did you observe something? So, here's a fun exercise for you, write down your observations, and find out the top 10 companies in real estate industry, in construction business, in cements, in hotels business, in malls, in ports, everything which is related to real estate and observe every company and find out why the first company by market cap is on first, where are others lagging behind, what is the first one doing extraordinary. This will increase your industrial knowledge of Real Estate industry, particularly in India that what works in India and what not.

Let me know tell how in my company process look like, so we are a in the business of selling the properties as I told you fix-and-flipping and BRRRR are my favorite strategies to apply and in my company, we sometimes do commit the builder beforehand and today with god's grace, we have enough money that we can commit, but in the beginning, I started like everyone else do, with zero or very less money, and with time, by applying strategies on 1, then 2, 3, 4 and so on properties, today there are many members in my team. So what our company do in real-time, let me give you a glimpse and quick look, summary of that. So, as I mentioned we are in the business of selling properties, so how our process looks like is:

The process of selling real estate in our company typically involves several key steps, including:

1. Marketing:

The first step in the process is to market the property to potential buyers. This may involve creating a listing for the property on the our website, advertising the property in local newspapers and magazines, online advertisements and hosting open houses or tours of the property.

2. Showing the property:

Once potential buyers express interest in the property, we will arrange for them to view the property. This may involve scheduling appointments for buyers to view the property or hosting open houses.

3. Negotiating offers:

After a potential buyer expresses interest in purchasing the property, we will negotiate with them to reach a mutually acceptable purchase price. This may involve counter-offers, contingencies, and other terms and conditions.

4. Due Diligence:

After a purchase agreement is reached, then the buyer will conduct due diligence on the property. This may involve obtaining a property inspection, reviewing title and other legal documents, and verifying that the property is in compliance with all relevant laws and regulations.

5. Closing:

Once due diligence is completed, the sale will be closed. This may involve signing a sales contract, transferring the title to the property, and paying closing costs.

6. Post Sale Services:

After the sale, we will often provide post-sale services such as property management, legal and documentation assistance, and other support services to the buyer. We, as a company, also give some special gift to our buyers. It makes them feel special and they always recommend our name to their friends and relatives.

It's important to note that different companies may have slightly different processes and procedures in place, and some companies may have additional steps or services that they offer. Additionally, different countries or jurisdictions may have different regulations and requirements that must be followed during the sale process.

CHAPTER EIGHT

Some Tips for Buying and Selling Properties

Tips for Buyers:

Buying a property can be a significant investment, and it's important to be well-informed and prepared before making a purchase. Here are some tips for buyers:

1. Get pre-approved for a mortgage:

Before you start looking for a property, it's a good idea to get pre-approved for a mortgage. This will give you an idea of how much you can afford to spend and will also make you a more attractive buyer to sellers.

2. Research the market:

Take the time to research the real estate market in the area where you're looking to buy. Look at prices of similar properties, check out property listings, and attend open houses to get a sense of what's available.

3. Hire a real estate agent:

A good real estate agent can help you navigate the buying process and can also provide valuable insight into the local market.

4. Get a home inspection:

Before making an offer on a property, it's a good idea to have a professional home inspector check the property for any potential issues.

5. Be prepared to negotiate:

Be prepared to negotiate with the seller on price, closing costs, and other terms of the sale.

6. Understand the legal aspect:

Real estate transactions have a lot of legalities, understand the legal aspects of buying, selling, leasing and renting property can help you navigate the complexities of the industry.

7. Take your time:

Don't rush into a purchase. Take your time to find the right property at the right price.

8. Consider the long-term:

Think about your future needs and plans, such as starting a family or planning for retirement.

By following these tips, buyers can make a more informed and confident decision when purchasing a property, and also be better prepared to navigate the process.

Tips for Sellers:

Selling a property can be a complex process, but by following these tips, you can increase your chances of a successful sale:

1. Price it right:

Pricing your property correctly is crucial to a successful sale. Research the prices of similar properties in your area, and consult with a real estate agent to determine a fair market value for your property.

2. Prepare your property for sale:

Make sure your property is in good condition and visually appealing. Consider making any necessary repairs or upgrades, and stage the property to make it more attractive to potential buyers.

3. Use professional photography and marketing materials:

High quality photographs and marketing materials can help your property stand out and attract more buyers.

4. Be flexible with showings:

Be willing to accommodate potential buyers' schedules and make it easy for them to view your property.

5. Be transparent:

Disclose any known issues with the property upfront, it will help maintain trust and credibility with potential buyers.

6. Get a home inspection:

A pre-inspection can help identify any issues with the property before they become a problem during the sales process.

7. Be open to negotiation:

Be prepared to negotiate with potential buyers and be willing to compromise to reach a deal that is mutually beneficial.

8. Work with a real estate agent:

A real estate agent can help you navigate the sales process, market your property to potential buyers, and negotiate on your behalf.

By following these tips, you can increase your chances of a successful sale and get the best possible price for your property.

These were some of the tips for the buyers and the sellers of properties.

CHAPTER NINE

Corruption in Indian Real Estate Industry

First, we have to learn about the taxes in India, while buying and selling a house. Let's see:

Taxes in Real Estate:

In India, taxes on real estate are typically made up of two main types: stamp duty and registration fee. **Stamp duty** is a tax on the transfer of ownership of property and is calculated as a percentage of the property's value. The **registration fee** is a charge for registering the sale of a property and is also a percentage of the property's value. The percentage rate for both of these taxes can vary depending on the state in which the property is located. Additionally, an annual property tax is also levied on the property owner by the local government.

We all know, Goods and Services Tax (GST) is a value-added tax that is applied to most goods and services in India. GST replaced several indirect taxes that were previously in place, such as VAT, service tax, and excise duty, with the aim of creating a unified, nationwide market. GST is applied at various rates, depending on the type of goods or services being supplied. For example, essential goods such as food and medicine have a lower GST rate, while luxury goods and services have a higher rate.

In the case of Real Estate, **GST** is applicable on under-construction properties, where the builder charges GST on the sale of the property instead of the stamp duty and registration fee. However, GST is not applicable on ready-to-move-in properties.

When selling real estate in India, the seller is responsible for paying capital gains tax on the profit from the sale. The tax rate for **long-term**

capital gains (property held for more than 24 months) is 20% with indexation (benefits) or 10% without indexation. **Short-term capital gains** (property held for less than 24 months) are taxed at the seller's applicable income tax slab/rate.

Additionally, we saw, the buyer is responsible for paying stamp duty and registration fees to the government. Here is one more kind of tax for seller, which is a part of STCG or LTCG, but it is deducted a little early (in/during transaction itself). **TDS (Tax Deducted at Source)** is applicable when selling real estate in India. As per Indian tax laws, TDS at the rate of 1% is required to be deducted by the buyer (which had to go to the seller) on the sale consideration of immovable property, if the consideration exceeds 50 Lakhs. The TDS so deducted needs to be deposited with the Indian government and the seller can claim credit for the same while filing their income tax returns. However, if the seller is able to produce a PAN card, the TDS rate is sometimes reduced to 0.25% for the same.

And currently, there are **no taxes on sale of agricultural land** in India.

These laws and tax slabs changes in budget, so keep an eye on Budget 2023 and you can consult a legal expert (CA in this case) to find taxes in your state and centre, which ones are applicable to you.

After this, let's now talk about **Corruption in Indian Real Estate market**, I remember one day, I saw a video on YouTube, made by **Sir Pranjal Kamra**, in which he talked about corruption in this sector in India. And it is a very true video, telling the reality of the market. And that day, I got inspired from that video, and thought that yes, I will also add this one section on corruption in Real Estate in India in my book. So, here it is. Let me now tell you about corruption in this sector in India:

If you belong to a middle class family, then just like those stock market stories, you must have heard these real estate stories from your parents as well, that if we had bought this property 15 years ago at Rs. 10-lakh, today it is worth Rs. 1.5 Crores. We, people, work all day so that we can purchase at least one home, our own home, that's why buying a house is not only a financial but an emotional decision as well, which we cannot solely do in an Excel sheet. Home is like an attachment to us, it has a deep impact on our emotions.

Let me tell you an incident, so we were about to sell our home, and as we did not have any emergency requirement of money, so we were getting a good deal, but when we started the process of selling, we found that all members of our family are not very happy. We had memories with that house. And specially my mom, were very sad, and then we were not able to do that deal. I know, it might sound very weird to some of you, but at that stage we chose our emotions and I think this was the best we could do there.

So, coming to corruption, we work all day and night, we save money, we cut our expenses, and do savings so that one day, we can also buy our own home. I know, some people actually sacrifice their entire life to buy a house and then if they are not able to buy, they blame themselves, but in reality, they are not at a fault. Property prices rise artificially due to corrupt people, and they become unaffordable for a common man.

Let's see how: So, for that purpose, let's take a property and call it A, so, let's say today, the price of A is Rs. 2 Crores. Let's say 10-15% tax is charged on it, when we buy it, so let's suppose we will get that property in Rs. 2.25 Crores (Taxes included) (If it's a ready-to-move property, 8-9% stamp duty and registration fees depending on which state you live, and if you buy an under-construction property, then 12-14% GST, again depending on some additional factors).

So, let's say XYZ is a corrupt person, and he had an income of around Rs. 20 crores this year, so after including all taxes(30% slab) + CESS + surcharges or any other charges, he will have to pay more than Rs. 8 Crores in taxes. (Now, everyone who is reading this, Please pay your taxes, they are for your benefit only. Government uses these taxes for people welfare (education, healthcare, infrastructure etc.)) Now, we know XYZ is a corrupt person, so to save these Rs. 8 Crores in taxes, he will show some business expenses while filing ITR, and will show a very little profit or zero profit to save from these taxes. Now, he has this black money Rs. 20 Crores, he will try to find some options, where he can invest these Rs. 20 Cr. Mostly, many capital markets like stock market etc. they cannot invest their black money there as it is connected with your PAN or bank account, so for settling this cash, only one or two capital markets are left for him as an option, and the main is Real Estate market, Here builder have to pay there workers (labor etc.) in cash, so they can easily settle and handle that cash.

So, they enter Real Estate and suppose that builder had made 15 homes/ flats of Rs. 2 Crore each, so this corrupt person says to him that he will buy 8 flats from him and give majority portion in cash. I talked about circle rate, when I explained some terms to you, So, it is the minimum rate at which the property is to be sold, it is decided by government.

Let's say that this property has a circle rate of Rs. 50 lakhs, so they decide that XYZ will buy this property at Rs. 50 lakhs from builder and other Rs.

1.5 Crore, he will give him in cash, in this way, here as well, when they go and register this property, builder have to pay 7-8% tax on these 50 lakhs, whereas you as a common man were paying this tax on Rs. 2 crores, so here is the another benefit for corrupt person, so he will invest more and more of his black money into real estate.

And he is paying in cash, so if the builder as well wanted a deal in cash, there is a possibility that the XYZ person will get some discount as well. So, this is a win-win situation for XYZ person. Now, from a builder's point of view, his 8 flats out of 15 are sold, so his investment is covered, now, he will hike the prices of the other left 7 flats from Rs. 2 crore to maybe Rs. 2.2 Crores and you as a common man will have to pay more now to buy that same flat.

This is how corruption rise prices of the properties as these corrupt people buy houses/flats in every city, state in every project, they capture most of the units with their black money, but the thing to note here is that, this is a very much simplified example, in reality these situations are more complex, but I just made you understand the core behind this.

Now, if this black money and corruption will get out from the Real Estate market, only then home prices would be affordable for a common man. And I truly believe that our government will definitely be taking some good initiatives like PMAY, RERA to improve the situation here as well.

CHAPTER TEN

Renting vs Buying a property

Oh! This is a never ending debate, man, Buy a house or Rent a house? So, I promise you one thing today that after reading this chapter, you will be able to make that decision for yourself, whether to buy or rent a home, by your own.

Now, I am not going to tell you in this section what is right or what is wrong, or do this, or what to do. Instead, I will be listing all the pros and cons of both sides so that you must know every parameter before making a decision, and you can make that decision on your own, but with some clarity that this is going to work for me, I do not know about the other people, but my requirements are this, so I will do this. So, let's now see how to make this decision and how to answer that toughest question of the world, i.e. Renting or Buying.

See, I can purely understand that buying a home is not only a financial decision, but an emotional decision as well. The comfort, safety, the good emotional feeling our own home gives us, you will not get that feeling anywhere else. But, for every emotion, there is a financial side as well. See, firstly, remember here, not any decision you will make is good or bad, you make it good or bad. In the last chapter where I told you that we did not sell my house due to my mother's emotions there, and that was a good decision, if we had sold that house, even that would be a good decision as well, but here is a catch. One is a good emotional decision, and one is a good financial decision. Now, let me not dig more into the philosophy side and bore you, let's directly see some pros and cons of both renting and buying a house.

The decision of whether to rent or buy a property is a personal one and depends on several factors including an individual's financial situation, lifestyle and long-term goals.

Here are some pros and cons of each option:

1. Renting:

First, let's talk about renting a house.

A. Pros:

a. Greater flexibility: Renting allows you to move around more easily, without the need to worry about selling a property.

b. Lower upfront costs: Renting typically requires less upfront capital, as you do not need to pay a down payment on a home.

c. Lower maintenance costs: Landlords are typically responsible for maintaining the property, so renters do not have to worry about the costs of repairs or renovations.

B. Cons:

a. No equity: Renting does not give you any equity in the property, as you are not building any wealth by paying your landlord's mortgage.

b. Limited control: Renters often have to abide by the rules set by the landlord and may not be able to make changes to the property.

c. Rent increases: Rent can increase over time, which can make it more difficult to budget for housing costs in the long-term.

2. Buying:

Now, let's talk about buying a house.

A. Pros:

a. Building equity: When you make a mortgage payment, you are building equity in the property, which can be used as a down payment on another property or as collateral for loans.

b. Tax benefits: Homeowners can deduct the interest they pay on their mortgage and property taxes on their income tax returns.

c. Sense of ownership: Owning a property can give you a sense of pride and stability, and you have the freedom to make changes to the property as you see fit.

B. Cons:

a. Higher upfront costs: Buying a property typically requires a significant amount of capital, including a down payment, closing costs, and other fees.

b. More responsibilities: As a homeowner, you are responsible for maintaining and repairing the property, which can be costly.

c. Limited flexibility: Buying a property means making a long-term commitment to a specific area, and it may be difficult or expensive to move if your circumstances change.

So, from here we can clearly see that renting offers greater flexibility, lower upfront costs and lower maintenance costs, while buying offers a sense of ownership, building equity and tax benefits. However, buying requires a significant amount of capital, more responsibilities and less flexibility. Before making a decision, it's important to consider your personal circumstances, including your financial situation, lifestyle, and long-term goals, and weigh the pros and cons of each option.

Still confused!? I know, it was just an introduction so that you can find the next part easy, now, let's quickly do some calculations and find out which is a better option.

So, before getting into all of this, let me tell you about rental yield, so it is the percentage of the property price which you are able to earn on rent every year.

So, for doing calculations in case of renting a home, we will reverse this term that how much of the property price we are paying to the owner i.e. how much is owner getting is reversed and viewed from our side. Actually, in India, on an average 2-3% is the residential rental yield, more near around 3%. At some places, it can be more, depending on city, location, and at some places it can be less as well, but on an average, the rental yield in residential real estate is 3%.

And one more thing, if any time, in India, (Actually it is very common in developed countries like the USA and the Canada etc. that their interest rates are very low, typically home loan interest rates are very low and even lower than the rental yield owners can get, so it is always the best choice there to buy a home as soon as you can, and you will always end up paying less EMIs than rent, if you choose it, but currently, it's all around the globe that interest rates are rising to control the inflation, I was not telling in the current scenario, but in general), it happens, never leave the golden chance. So, it is a kind of arbitrage opportunity, not exactly, but kind of, and that's why it will disappear very soon to keep the market in symmetry and efficient, competitive.

And also, for quick calculations, you can use the 4-4.5% rental yield rule according to your definitions. That, if rental yield on a house is less than 4-4.5%, then you can continue living on rent there and if it is more, then you can think of buying that property. Rental yield is simply you will get by dividing annual rent by price of the property and multiply it by 100, then check 4-4.5% rule according to your preferences.

Let's now talk about the two views of seeing this topic and see some detailed calculation:

1. *Financial View:*

So, for seeing this situation from a financial perspective, we need to enter into an Excel sheet and check whether, with normal assumptions, what is better, renting or buying. So, I will be taking the average of everything which is going on in the market right now i.e. I will be taking rental yield as 3%, Property appreciation as 6%, rate of return on investments as 10% (taking a lower side in SIP, for safety purposes), so let's see with an example (general). And then you can change these rates as per you are getting in your case and see the difference it made and try to check that in your case as well, what is the better financial decision for you, let's see now for a general case:

Number of Years	20	Number of Years	20
RENT		BUY	
Monthly Rent	25,000	Cost of Property	10,000,000
Tax Benefit	10%	Downpayment	15%
Effective Rent	22,500	Downpayment Amount	1,500,000
Annual Rent	270,000	Loan Amount	8,500,000
		Interest rate for Loan	7%
Average Annual Rental Increment	6%	Loan Duration	20
Total Rent for the period	**9,932,110**	EMI	65,900
		Tax Bracket	10%
Downpayment Amount	1,500,000	Effective Interest rate for Loan	6.3%
Saving in Monthly EMI	39,877	Effective EMI	62,377
Rate of Return on investment	10%	Total Net Interest Paid over the period	6,470,447
		Maintenance Cost	0.30%
Value of Downpayment saved	10,992,110	Maintenance Amount	2,500
Value of EMI saved	30,281,246	Annual Increase in Maintenance	4%
		Total Maintenance over the period	916,937
Net Benefit of Renting a House	**31,341,246**		
		Total Cost of Buying the House	**17,387,383**
Net Difference (Benefit of Renting- Benefit of Buying)		Increase in Property Value	6%
is greater than 0, Hence, Renting is better than		Value of Property after the period	32,071,355
buying a house in this case.		**Net Benefit of Buying a House**	**14,683,971**

Excel Sheet (Renting vs Buying Calculation)

So, for an example, let's consider that you are going to stay in a specific city or in a specific locality for the next 20 years so, you want to decide whether you should stay in a rented house, or you buy a house? Now, Assume that the monthly rent for the house that you are looking at is Rs. 25000/- Typically, you know, today, in an above-average locality for 2 and a half or 3BHK, this would be a nominal rent. I am also assuming that you are into the 10% tax slab. Therefore, you will get HRA (House Rent Allowance) benefit, so, your effective rent payment is going to be Rs. 22500/- Now if I take it on an annual basis, Rs. 22500 multiplied by 12 is Rs. 2,70,000/- Hence, it is your annual rental amount. And let's also assume that the average annual rental increment is 6%, then the total rent for 20 years is Rs. 99,32,110/-

Now, let's see the second option, which is buying a house. So, for that purpose, we are considering the same kind of house in the same kind of locality and almost the same factors to avoid complexity. Let's assume that the price of the property is Rs. 1 Crores, and if you want to buy it, assuming that you will be paying 15% as the down payment and other for financing the other 85%, you will take a bank loan at 7% interest rate. Again, for simplicity, we assume that the loan duration is also 20 years so that we can compare these two different cases. So, your EMI will be Rs. 65,900/- (This everything I have calculated in the Excel sheet is by using some formulas, concepts and methods from this financial concept "Time value of money", at some places, I calculate future value, present value, at some places EMI i.e. annuity, so I used those methods) in this case. So, you were in the 10% tax bracket, therefore, the effective rate of interest for your loan will be 6.3% after taking into consideration the tax benefits. Therefore, your effective EMI will turn out to Rs. 62,377/- Again, let's assume that you will be paying 0.3% maintenance charges which is Rs. 2500/- And Of course, every society will increase the maintenance every year, so I have taken that increase as 4% Hence, your total maintenance over the period of 20 years will be Rs. 9,16,937/- So, what is your total cost of buying the house? It is the total cost of your property plus the effective interest on the loan plus the total maintenance charges which sums up to Rs. 1,73,87,383/-

Now, The most important part here is decision-making. Let's see that once for this general case. So, if you decide to go with the renting option, what will happen? First, you will save on the down payment, Rs. 15 lakhs.

Second, your effective EMI was Rs.62,377/- in case of buying, now you will only pay the effective rent which was Rs. 22,500/- saving you Rs.39877/- [i.e. 62,377-22,500] So, you have a lump-sum of Rs. 15 lakhs saved, and also the monthly saving is Rs. 39,877/- Now assume that you are investing this amount at 10% CAGR for the next 20 years. The value of the down payment saved will become Rs. 1,09,92,110/- after 20 years, and this monthly EMI saved will become Rs. 3,02,81,246/- So, your net benefit of renting a house will be the sum of these two minus the total rent (Rs. 99,32,110/-) for 20 years, which is coming to be Rs. 3,13,41,246/-. That is what I did in the Excel sheet.

Now, Let's see the other case and try to find out the net benefit in case of buying a house. So, let's assume that you will get an appreciation on the house on an average of 6% for 20 years. So, your property of Rs.1 Crore will become Rs. 3,20,71,355/- Therefore, the net benefit of buying the house will be the future property price minus the original cost of buying it, where the original cost is the total cost of buying it, plus interest amount plus maintenance charges. So, your net benefit will be Rs. 1,46,83,971/- in this case of buying a house as I calculated in the Excel sheet given above.

So, your net benefit in case of renting a house was Rs. 3.13 Crores and your net benefit in case of buying a house is Rs. 1.4 Crores. So, here we can see a clear and a big difference in the net benefits. So, according to the financial view, it generally makes sense to rent a house. But, a thing to note here is that, this was a very general example and things can be very much different in the reality, you can get 8% property appreciation etc., so all these assumptions, if we change them, then there are some possibilities that this decision might change, but as we saw, it genuinely makes financial sense to rent a house in this general case particularly, emotionally, we will see it in the next section.

2. Emotional View:

If you ask your gym trainer whether you can eat momos or not, he/she will not allow you, if you ask a doctor in winters whether you can eat an ice-cream or not, he/she will not allow you, and if you ever ask a financial expert, whether to buy or rent a house, he will open up that Excel sheet that we just saw in the above section, but we are not robots that work on only scientific, mathematical and logical things. The thing which separates us from these machines, is our Emotions.

And a middle class person can feel the importance of having their own home, the people who have lived their childhood in a rental home, they can as well understand the importance of having their own home. And if they want to live this feeling of having their own home, then there's nothing wrong in that. So, the point is, correct answer to this question depends on you, what you want, your mental peace and yes, of course you need to take care of the financial side as well, not only emotions. So, it's a different answer for everyone, and I hope you find that soon.

In Conclusion, these were the all factors which will help you decide whether you should buy or rent a house, and remember, this is an individual decision. You can assign as much weights to those factors of your choice as much you like. All the best, Make a good decision!

Overview and Future Trends of Real Estate Sector in India

Overview of Real Estate Sector (To be Industry) in India

The real estate industry in India is a rapidly growing sector that plays a significant role in the country's economy. The industry is driven by factors such as population growth, urbanization, and rising disposable incomes. The Indian real estate market is broadly divided into many segments but two main segments are: residential and commercial. The residential segment includes the construction and sale of apartments, villas, and independent houses. The commercial segment includes the construction and sale of office buildings, retail spaces, and warehouses.

The Indian government has taken several steps in recent years to boost the real estate industry, including the implementation of the Real Estate (Regulation and Development) Act (RERA) in 2016, which aims to protect the rights of property buyers and promote transparency in the sector. Additionally, the government has announced various schemes such as Pradhan Mantri Awas Yojana to provide affordable housing to the economically weaker sections of society.

The Indian real estate market has been affected by the global pandemic in 2020, with a decline in sales and new launches. However, the market is expected to recover in the coming years as the economy rebounds and demand for housing and commercial spaces increases.

The real estate industry in India is a significant contributor to the country's economy. The Indian real estate sector also has an important role in the country's employment generation and GDP contribution. According to data from the Ministry of Housing and Urban Affairs, the industry is valued at around $180 billion and is expected to grow to $1 trillion by 2030.

Hence, the sector is expected to grow at a CAGR of 11% till 2030. The sector is also a major employer in the country, providing jobs to millions of people involved in construction, sales, and management. The construction sector alone is expected to generate around 30 million jobs in the next decade. The real estate sector is also a major contributor to India's GDP, accounting for around 6-7% of the country's GDP.

In terms of investment, the Indian real estate sector attracted around $8 billion of foreign direct investment (FDI) between April 2000 and December 2019. The government has also announced plans to make it easier for foreign investors to invest in the Indian real estate market by relaxing the rules for foreign direct investment (FDI).

This was the current state of Real Estate market.

Understanding Real Estate Market in India and some Future Trends and Opportunities:

The real estate industry in India is a rapidly growing sector. When we look around the globe that what is happening in other economies, we get to know that different countries are showing different trends right now in real estate. Some developed countries like the USA and the Canada are in uptrend, Dubai is just coming from a downtrend and is looking to recover as it is showing some uptrend indications, and the best chance in real estate currently is with our country India.

After remaining stagnant for almost eight years, now there is the time of completion of this cycle and the trend to change in upside direction. Now, the real estate market will be showing rapid growth in some sectors, according to me, I will give some reasons as well. So, let's start.

See, Real estate has a longer cycle, unlike stocks or some other assets with short cycles. A typical real estate cycle goes on for 8–10 years. If you know, we just got out of a boom in 2013-14 in Indian real estate market and then went into a downward cycle. It is approximated till 2022 and then now, there is time for a turnaround, to go up.

Overviewing industry, we had an unsold inventory of 12 lakh properties unsold in 2018-19, which was the peak. It was 5 years stock. In only Mumbai region, there were 2 lakh units unsold and in Delhi NCR region, 3 lakh units were unsold during that time. But then, the pandemic happened, and it worked as a blessing in disguise for our real estate industry. During the

Covid-19 pandemic, our Indian government comes with some very good schemes for real estate sector. They offered some reduction in the taxes, stamp duty, and helped clear out this huge stock and all their strategies worked beautifully. A record sale was made, Out of those unsold 2 lakh units, the 1 lakh units were sold in Mumbai alone in one single year. And therefore the demand started increasing but, now, there were some supply constraints as the new addition to number of properties were less, and our stock came from five years to three years. Now, we all know the completion time of a project is about approximately 3 to 5 years, so the current situation may create some scarcity in a few years. That's why this is the best time to enter the real estate market in India. As when this left stock is sold out, but the next level of supply has not come out yet, then the prices will skyrocket.

So, a real estate boom is expected to be start by 2023. So, today is the best time to enter the real estate sector.

Next, the residential rental income was about 2% in 2018, and now it is around 4%. As the interest rates are increasing, inflation is increasing, the rental yields will definitely rise as well around 6%, so the future is bright in the real estate sector for property owners. One more good thing that happened for owners is the Model Tenant Act, 2021. This act will protect the interest of property owners.

So, now there is a separate regulatory authority for this, which will take less time. If you need possession, now you will be able to get that within six months. So this assures investor's interests and rental yield is also rising, so there is a win-win opportunity by investing in real estate. In my opinion, the best locations to bet for next decade in residential real estate are Hyderabad, Pune and the outskirts of Bangalore as well.

Also, today there are visible changes in our Indian real estate sector, it is a more regulated industry now, investors are secured now. Safe funds like retirement funds, pension funds, Private Equity companies are entering into the Real estate market of India which is making this sector organized. We have seen REITs as well.

Next, the commercial real estate typically gives a rental income equal to the sum of rate of interest (on fixed deposits or government bonds) + 2 to 4%, making it around 8-12% rental yield. Now, easily there will be 5% increase every year. The thing with commercial properties are they give higher rentals around 8-10% (on an average), but give less capital appreciation, whereas the residential properties give higher capital appreciation but lesser rental yield. But yes, residential do provide some better income tax benefits as well.

Now, there are REITs today which typically invest in offices, which they give on leases for long term (Maybe around 10–15 years). In REITs as well, rental income and capital appreciation both are almost assured, and they are easy to buy and sell as well. REITs provide very easy entry and exit to real estate market with no GST, stamp duty etc. but yes it generally gives a lower rate of return, around 10-12% including capital appreciation.

And you know what is the beauty of commercial real estates, good commercial properties can be found in every city, at any place, where there are footfalls. So, in my opinion, this decade, the Real Estate industry in India will dominate.

Now, During covid, we see a rapid change in residential real estates, due to this work from home, people were more interested in buying 2bhk+ 1 extra bedroom (for their work). As they will get this at a price less than 3bhk for sure. So, many people were preferring this type of homes.

Next, during this time, the concept of CBD is losing its importance and a new Hub and spoke model is gaining some great traction. Unlike before, today companies, people like to have five to six small offices in the different parts of city, instead of that one big office near CBD. So, now, these commercial properties between the residential areas affecting the prices of residential properties in a good way as well.

Next is, now-a-days, there is one more kind of properties in demand, that is a special (separate) housing requirement for old people. Now, that can be one extra bedroom in the home or other requirements as well. Senior citizens living is the new trend, Day care centers are opening and all these things are giving good positive signals to the real estate industry. I will try to explain in more detail about the silver economy and its impact on Indian real estate now and how it will give India a great boom in real estate. We will see that. Also, old age homes are becoming outdated, old age living is the new trend (in which all healthcare etc. facilities are included).

Also, some concepts like home-sharing and co-ownership, service-cum-real estate, time-sharing are also getting started. Let me give you an example. Suppose there is a person A, who is a bachelor and just started earning, his earnings are okay, but he is single now, so he wants only one private room and some common space can work, similarly, there are other people like him as well, so what they can do, 3 people can together buy/rent a 3bhk and share the rent, there as well service-cum-real estate is being popular, and many companies are doing it now.

Also, some people do need their homes to live for some days only, so they are trying the concepts of Airbnb etc. which is providing them with an additional income. Also, it is an observable trend that the private equity companies majorly invest in those real estates which can be hostels for students, or they can be made into PGs etc. because this way, they can earn more and can increase their rental yield.

Now, after getting a glimpse and understanding some insights about this industry, let's now see, what are some future trends and opportunities:

PropTech:

This is one of the most promising trends out there. PropTech (property technology) refers to the use of technology to improve and innovate processes and services in the real estate industry. This can include everything from online platforms for buying and selling property, to the use of data analytics and building management systems to improve the efficiency and sustainability of buildings. Some examples of propTech include online real estate marketplaces, virtual and augmented reality tools for property viewings, and smart home technology for building management. We have talked about this in a lot of detail in the PropTech section.

Warehousing:

This is again one of the most promising trends out there, the next big thing in India is going to be warehouses. Warehousing has been an increasingly important trend in the real estate industry in recent years. This is primarily due to the growth of e-commerce and the need for more storage and distribution space to meet the demands of online shoppers.

The trend of e-commerce has been a major driver of warehouse demand. As more and more consumers are shopping online, retailers and logistics companies are in need of more warehouse space to store and ship products. This has led to an increase in the construction of new warehouses and the conversion of existing industrial buildings into modern, high-tech facilities. The trend for larger and more efficient warehouses is also growing. Many companies are seeking out larger facilities with higher ceilings, more loading docks, and better access to transportation in order to improve their supply chain operations.

Another trend is the growing popularity of multi-level warehouses. These facilities are designed to maximize the use of space by stacking storage levels on top of each other, and they can be a more cost-effective option for companies that need a lot of storage space in a relatively small area.

Overall, the increasing demand for warehouse space is expected to continue as e-commerce continues to grow, and more goods are being bought and sold online. As a result, the warehousing and logistics sector is becoming an increasingly important part of the real estate industry, and investors are increasingly looking at this sector as a source of growth and income.

Data Centres:

Next in the list, we have are, Data Centres. If you have keenly observed, you must have seen that these companies like Google, IBM are buying out spaces in India for making big data centers. And I think, in this budget 2023, there will be some incentive for these as well. Because Indian government is concerned about our security, so they want that data of Indian people should be stores in Indian data centers or the data centers in India itself, that's why we have seen this very recently.

So, Data centers are a growing trend in the real estate industry as the need for data storage and processing continues to increase. Data centers are facilities that house servers and other computing equipment for the storage, management, and dissemination of data. They are critical for the functioning of many industries, including technology, finance, healthcare, and government.

The growth in data centers is driven by several factors, including the increasing amount of data being generated and stored, the growing use of cloud computing, and the need for faster and more reliable data processing. As a result, data centers are becoming an increasingly important part of the real estate industry. The increasing demand for data centers has led to the construction of new facilities and the conversion of existing buildings into data centers. This has led to increased investment in the industry and has created new opportunities for real estate developers, landlords, and investors. The impact of data centers on the real estate industry can be significant, particularly in the commercial property market. Data centers often require large, specialized facilities that can be expensive to construct and maintain. This can lead to higher rental rates and property values in areas where data centers are located.

Additionally, data centers can also have a positive impact on the local economy by creating jobs and generating tax revenue. In terms of environmental impact, data centers consume a large amount of energy and can have a large carbon footprint, so there is a growing trend in the industry to make data centers more energy efficient and sustainable.

Overall, the increasing trend of data centers is expected to continue to have a significant impact on the real estate industry, creating opportunities for real estate developers, landlords, and investors, as well as impacting the commercial property market.

Blockchain in real estate:

Blockchain technology has the potential to revolutionize the way real estate transactions are conducted and recorded by creating tamper-proof digital ledger of property ownership and transaction history. The use of blockchain in real estate can help to improve transparency, security and efficiency in various aspects of the real estate industry.

One of the main use cases of blockchain in real estate is in property title management. Blockchain-based property title management systems can create a digital record of property ownership that is secure and tamper-proof. This can help to reduce the risk of fraud and errors in property transactions and make it easier for buyers and sellers to verify ownership and transfer titles.

Another use case of blockchain in real estate is in property transactions. Blockchain-based real estate platforms can enable buyers and sellers to conduct transactions directly, without the need for intermediaries such as real estate agents or escrow services. This can help to reduce costs and improve the efficiency of property transactions.

Blockchain technology can also enable smart contracts, which are digital contracts that can be executed automatically when certain conditions are met. Smart contracts can be used in real estate to automate the process of buying and selling property, such as transferring title and funds when a sale is complete. In addition, blockchain technology can also enable tokenization of real estate assets, where a property is divided into digital tokens that can be bought and sold like stocks, enabling fractional ownership and liquidity.

Overall, blockchain technology has the potential to transform the real estate industry by increasing transparency, security, and efficiency in property transactions and title management. It is still an emerging technology, and it's important to note that its implementation has challenges like regulatory compliance, standardization, and adoption by the industry players.

The silver economy and the real estate:

Now, this is that trend about which I was talking above. This is going to boom our real estate sector soon. The silver economy refers to the economic activity generated by the aging population, particularly those over the age of 60. The real estate industry can play a significant role in the silver economy by providing housing and other related services that meet the needs of older adults.

One of the main ways that the real estate industry can support the silver economy is by providing age-friendly housing. This can include features such as accessibility, safety, and security, as well as community amenities that promote social engagement and active living. There are also specific housing models such as "assisted living" or "memory care" facilities that are designed to meet the specific needs of older adults.

Another way that the real estate industry can support the silver economy is by providing services such as home care and home modification. These services can help older adults to continue living in their own homes as they age, rather than needing to move into a care facility. This can be beneficial for both older adults and their families, as it allows them to maintain their independence and autonomy, while also reducing the costs of long-term care.

In addition, real estate developers are also exploring ways to create age-friendly communities that offer a range of services and amenities that meet the needs of older adults. This can include things like transportation, health care services, and social and recreational activities, all of which can help older adults to maintain a high quality of life.

The real estate industry can play a critical role in the silver economy by providing housing and related services that meet the needs of older adults. By creating age-friendly housing, home care and home modification services, and age-friendly communities, real estate developers can help to support the well-being and independence of older adults.

How Climate Change is impacting the real estate sector?

Next, we are now going to see how Climate change will impact this sector. Climate change can have a significant impact on the real estate industry. Rising sea levels, more intense storms, and other weather-related events can damage or destroy property. Changes in temperature and precipitation patterns can also affect the livability and desirability of certain areas.

As a result, property values in areas that are at higher risk of flooding or other climate-related damage may decrease, while values in areas that are considered less vulnerable may increase. This can lead to changes in property tax revenues, insurance rates, and mortgage availability.

In addition, the industry may also see increased demand for properties that are more energy efficient and resilient to climate change-related risks. This could include homes with solar panels, green roofs, or other sustainable features. Real estate developers and investors must consider the impact of climate change on their projects, to ensure they are not investing in areas that are likely to be affected by natural disasters or other risks. They may also need to invest more money in building stronger, more resilient structures that can better withstand extreme weather events.

Overall, the real estate industry will have to adapt to the impact of climate change, by creating new products and services that help mitigate its risks and creating new standards and regulations that ensure properties are built to withstand future weather extremes.

Next, I think there will be a question in some people's mind i.e. **Is Emigration possible with the help of real estate,** so let me answer this.

Real estate can play a role in emigration, as individuals and families may choose to purchase property in another country as a way to establish a new home and potentially gain citizenship or residency status. This is known as "investor immigration" or "citizenship by investment" programs.

Many countries, such as Canada, the United States, and those in the European Union, offer various types of investor immigration programs to foreign nationals who are willing to invest a certain amount of money in the country's real estate, business or other assets. These programs can provide a path to permanent residency or citizenship for the investor and their family.

Real estate agents and developers in these countries may target foreign investors looking for investment immigration opportunities. Additionally, there are also specialized agents, lawyers, and consultants that provide guidance and assistance in the process of obtaining a residence permit or citizenship through real estate investment.

However, it's worth noting that these types of programs can be quite expensive and may have strict requirements and criteria for eligibility. Additionally, it's important to research the legal requirements, tax implications and the political stability of the country you are considering immigrating to.

And at last, I did a comparison between the real estate markets of the USA, the Canada, the Dubai and the India. Let's see that.

Real Estate Market in India vs USA vs Dubai vs Canada:

The real estate markets in the United States, Canada, Dubai, and India are all quite different and have their own unique characteristics.

The United States has a large and diverse real estate market, with a wide range of property types and prices. The market is primarily driven by economic conditions and interest rates, and is currently experiencing a strong recovery from the impact of the COVID-19 pandemic. Housing prices have been rising in many areas, especially in larger cities such as New York and San Francisco.

Canada also has a diverse real estate market, with a mix of urban and rural properties. The market is driven by economic conditions and immigration, with prices in major cities like Toronto and Vancouver being higher than in other parts of the country. The market has also been impacted by the pandemic, but has been recovering and rising right now.

Dubai's real estate market is primarily driven by tourism and foreign investment. Dubai has become a popular destination for real estate investment, as it offers a relatively stable political environment, tax-free income, and a strong rental market. However, the market has been affected by the pandemic, with a decrease in demand and an oversupply of properties. But, right now their market is recovering at a good pace, showing some uptrend and giving a turnaround.

India's real estate market is diverse and rapidly growing, driven by urbanization and a growing middle class. However, it's also been affected by economic downturns and a lack of clear regulations, leading to a slowdown in sales and a build-up of unsold inventory in some areas. The Indian real estate market has also been impacted by the pandemic, with a decrease in demand and an oversupply of properties. And similar to Dubai, India's real estate market is starting its rise, and it will keep growing now for this cycle. 2023 possibly be the best recovery time for our market, and it will show some uptrends here as well.

In general, each of these markets has its own unique characteristics and is driven by different factors. It's important to understand the specific (property) market conditions in the area you are interested to invest in.

CHAPTER TWELVE

Different Asset Classes and Comparison with Real Estate

Asset Classes

There are several different types of asset classes in the world, including:

1. Cash and cash equivalents: This includes assets such as savings accounts, money market funds, and short-term government bonds that can be easily converted into cash.

2. Bonds: These are debt securities issued by companies, municipalities, and governments. When you buy a bond, you are lending money to the issuer in exchange for regular interest payments and the return of principal at maturity. These both can also be termed as Fixed-income instruments.

3. Stocks: Also known as **Equities**, stocks represent ownership in a company. When a company issues stock, it is raising capital in exchange for a share of the company. As a shareholder, you have the potential to earn money through dividends and capital appreciation. The value of your investment can increase or decrease depending on performance of the company and the stock market as a whole.

4. Real estate: It refers to the ownership or use of land and buildings. When you invest in real estate, you are buying a property, such as a house or a commercial building. The value of your investment can increase or decrease depending on the real estate market and the specific property you have invested in. This includes many types of commercial, residential, others etc. properties, such as office buildings, apartments, and houses. Real estate can generate income through rent and appreciation.

5. Commodities: This includes raw materials such as precious metals, oil, and agricultural products. Commodities can be traded on commodity exchanges, and their value can fluctuate based on supply and demand.

6. Alternative investments: This is a catch-all category that includes assets such as paintings, real estate is also a part of alternative investments, there are some new emerging assets as well, like cryptocurrencies, NFTs which do not fit into the traditional asset classes. These investments tend to be more complex and less liquid than traditional investments.

Each asset class has its own unique set of risks and potential returns, and different investors may have different preferences for which types of assets they want to include in their portfolios.

But let me give you a quick comparison between all these assets on the basis of risk and return. Remember this rule of finance, **where risk increases, the expected return will also increase**. Capital Asset pricing model is a good example of this rule.

So, I will now show you these assets arranged in an order from lowest to highest risky, that means the expected return will also be increasing in that order.

Let's see now: Here is a list of asset classes from lowest to highest risk:

1. Government Bonds: Government bonds are considered to be low-risk investments as they are issued by governments, which typically have a lower default risk than other issuers. The returns on government bonds are generally lower than equity or real estate, but they are considered to be more stable and predictable.

2. Cash and cash equivalents: This includes assets such as savings accounts, money market funds, and short-term government bonds that can be easily converted into cash. These are considered to be low-risk investments, but also have low returns.

3. Gold: Gold has traditionally been considered a safe haven asset, as its value tends to hold up well during times of economic uncertainty. However, gold prices can be affected by changes in interest rates, currency fluctuations and other factors. Gold investment is considered less risky than equity, but returns on gold investment are generally lower than equity.

4. Bonds: These are debt securities issued by companies, municipalities, and governments. When you buy a bond, you are lending money to the issuer in exchange for regular interest payments and the return of principal at maturity. Bonds are considered less risky than equity investments, but more risky than cash and gold investments.

5. Real Estate: Real estate investments can generate income through rent and appreciation. However, the value of real estate can be affected by local and national economic conditions, as well as changes in interest rates. Real estate investments are generally considered to be less risky than equity investments but more risky than government bonds, cash and gold investments.

6. Stocks (Equity): Stocks represent ownership in a company and have the potential for high returns, but also come with a higher level of risk. The value of your investment can increase or decrease depending on the performance of the company and the stock market as a whole. Historically, equities have provided higher returns over the long term, but also come with higher volatility and hence considered more risky than other asset classes.

7. Alternative investments: This is a catch-all category that includes assets, such as cryptocurrency like Blockchain, Ethereum, which do not fit into the traditional asset classes. These investments tend to be more complex than traditional investments and usually considered as high-risk investments.

It's important to note that the level of risk of an investment can vary depending on the specific investment and the investor's individual risk tolerance.

One last thing here, I want to tell is, some people ask me **how much of our portfolio should be invested in real estate?** So, There is no one-size-fits-all answer to how much of a person's portfolio should be invested in real estate. It depends on an individual's financial goals, risk tolerance, and overall investment strategy. However, as a general rule of thumb, it is recommended to diversify investments across different asset classes and industries to spread out the risk. Real estate can be a great addition to a diversified portfolio. It can provide a steady stream of rental income and the potential for long-term appreciation.

I think, a good starting point would be to allocate 10-20% of a portfolio to real estate. However, this can vary depending on the individual's circumstances and goals. Some investors may choose to invest more in real estate if they believe that the real estate market is favorable, and they have a good understanding of the market. Others may choose to invest less if they prefer to have a more diversified portfolio.

It's important to consult with your financial advisor to determine the appropriate allocation of real estate in your portfolio, taking into account your unique financial situation and goals